SOUTHEAST
Foraging

SOUTHEAST
Foraging

120 wild and flavorful edibles
from angelica to wild plums

CHRIS BENNETT

TIMBER PRESS
Portland, Oregon

Timber Press
Workman Publishing
Hachette Book Group, Inc.
1290 Avenue of the Americas
New York, New York 10104
timberpress.com

Timber Press is an imprint of Workman Publishing, a division of Hachette Book Group, Inc. The Timber Press name and logo are registered trademarks of Hachette Book Group, Inc.

Printed in China on responsibly sourced paper
Eleventh printing 2024
Text and cover design by Benjamin Shaykin

The publisher is not responsible for websites (or their content) that are not owned by the publisher.

The Hachette Speakers Bureau provides a wide range of authors for speaking events. To find out more, go to hachettespeakersbureau.com or email HachetteSpeakers@hbgusa.com.

Library of Congress Cataloging-in-Publication Data

Bennett, Chris, 1979– author.
    Southeast foraging: 120 wild and flavorful edibles from angelica to wild plums/Chris Bennett.—First edition.
        pages cm
    Includes bibliographical references and index.
    ISBN 978-1-60469-499-4
    1. Wild plants, Edible—Southern States. 2. Forage plants—Southern States. I. Title.
    QK98.5.U6B45 2015
    581.6'320975—dc23   2014038439

To my father, Tom Bennett, who first taught me about foraging.

Contents

Foraging in the Southeast

Foraging for wild edibles is undergoing a renaissance in the United States. Whether it is the logical extension of the farm-to-table movement or the result of decades of American reforestation, foraging is an experience no longer claimed just by hunters and campers. We are living in a fortunate moment when you might find local edible wild plants on your dinner table at an urban restaurant. You might be able to take a community foraging class taught by a local expert who lives in your neighborhood. You may even find yourself in your own backyard plucking some wild ginger for your morning tea or gathering dandelion greens for the evening's salad.

This rebirth of interest in edible wild plants is good for the landscape and for preserving our cultural heritage. Foraged foods require no packaging, spraying, or fertilizing to be at their freshest and most tasty. They need no trucking or shipping to reach your table, for this is as close to the land as you can eat. From the mountains of West Virginia and the Carolinas to the swamps of Louisiana and the coastal floodplains of Mississippi and Alabama, the Southeast is extremely rich and diverse in wild edibles. Wild plants are copious in wild lands; no logging, clearing, or plowing is required to create optimal growing conditions for these edibles. At the same time, this free food is available in all types of landscapes—urban, suburban, rural. The range of different plant habitats in the Southeast is staggering: mountains, foothills, plateaus, floodplains, swamps, marshes, grasslands, forests, ridges, valleys, lawns, meadows, overgrown fields, thickets, disturbed soil, seashores, riverbanks, lakes, and bogs. This makes foraging accessible to everyone, in every part of the region and within every budget. For many folks who are eager to reconnect with heritage cooking and lifestyles, foraging also offers a direct link to the past. Those hickory nuts and that garlic mustard you might find today are the same ingredients early Native Americans and European settlers were gathering for their own meals in days long ago.

Foraged foods are good for our bellies, too. Distinctively wild flavors are adding a new dimension to American regional cuisines. No one knows this as well as chefs in the Southeast, who recently have been cooking with and seeking out traditional and foraged foods with enthusiasm. Growing up in Alabama on my family's farm gave me a strong connection to the land of my region. I did not fully

Flowers of the maypop vine give way to citrus-flavored fruit in late summer.

realize this relationship until after I returned home from cooking in restaurants in Chicago and other big cities. Reading agrarian writers like Wendell Berry and chefs like Michel Bras gave me a strong reestablished awareness of the region's food ways. I wanted to provide and revive the almost lost knowledge of foraging for wild edibles for the restaurant scene and home kitchen.

I supply restaurants in Birmingham, Alabama, with wild edibles throughout the year. I love walking through the back door of a restaurant carrying the first wild strawberries of the year and seeing how everyone's eyes light up as the glorious sight and aroma of the berries fill the room. I also truly enjoy teaching classes on foraging to people in the area. They generally are surprised and delighted at the bounty that the Southeast has to offer. I get so much pleasure just spreading the word about all the wild foods that are around us and how much fun it is to seek them out.

I've written this book so you can quickly and easily find what you need to know about wild edible plants in the Southeast. In the first section, I introduce you to the world of foraging, and offer detailed information on where to forage in our region, how to identify the edible plants, what equipment you might need, and the ethics of foraging. The next section lists what wild edibles are available for gathering, by season and habitat, from mountains to seashore. Then, the majority of the book presents plant profiles that are listed alphabetically. Each plant entry introduces the plant's features and edible parts, includes photographs for identification, and offers tips for gathering, preparing, and preserving each edible.

So, come take a walk with me through the pine forests, coastal plains, and hilly uplands of our southeastern states and let's see what we will find.

Foraging:
An Introduction

I often get asked, Why do you forage? I forage because I love how rich and diverse nature is in the South and I love food. Foraging leads you to delicious, nutritious wild foods, is sustainable, and helps you to be a more creative cook.

Unique tastes and textures of wild edibles

From the sour tartness of sumac to the citrusy, grapefruitlike aroma of Virginia pine needles, wild edible plants offer flavors and textures you cannot find in local supermarkets. That is one of the reasons that chefs seek them out. They also relish using them because they want their food to reflect the local environment.

Many weeds that you often walk by are tasty and even appear on restaurant menus

Overgrown fields are one of my favorite places to forage because of the abundance of wild edibles they harbor.

and sometimes even in farmers' market stalls. Pokeweed, wood sorrel, field garlic, and purslane are just a few of those.

Food that money can't buy

Free food is all around us. Foraging is not just for survivalists; it's also a fun way to supplement your diet.

Some cultivated crops, like strawberries, originated in the wild. Over time, strawberries to be trucked to market were bred to be bigger and tougher, and to have more consistent yields; the result is a berry that is big and brawny, yes, but less flavorful, less aromatic. The wild versions are small but intensely flavored. They are also free and taste better than any commercial variety.

Knowledge about nature

People often tell me that if they were in a survival situation, they would want me on their team. Foraging is a skill that is enjoyable and also valuable. It's comforting to know how much food is out there. My grandparents' generation who grew up in the Depression knew how to forage—they did it out of necessity.

When you read this book, you will gain critical knowledge about the plants around you. I hope you will pass on this knowledge. Foraging has almost become a lost art.

Foraging is fun!

I love to forage because it is fun! You never know what you might find. You may come home with an empty basket, or you may discover some stinging nettles. Foraging is sort of like collecting antiques. No matter where you are traveling, you are always looking for new and exciting findings.

Environmental impact

Foraging has an important impact on the world around us. It is possible to be irresponsible when foraging and overharvest a plant to the point where it will not grow back. On the other hand, many plants are extremely invasive so foraging helps to control them.

A love of the land

If you love the landscape of your area, you want to learn about it. Foraging is a great way to do this. When you forage in a place for several years, you learn weather patterns and how they affect the growth of wild edible plants. This knowledge comes in handy when a chef is asking you about how the wild blackberry crop is doing.

Foraging helps you connect with nature directly because you are interacting with it. You are becoming intimately familiar with the landscape you are in. I may live in the city, but every time I walk along a sidewalk and I spy chickweed or dandelion greens, the world opens up in front of me.

Foraging Ethics and Sustainability

There is a golden rule in foraging: Never take everything. There are a few exceptions, but as a forager, you need to understand your impact on your world. It is important to learn how to forage sustainably. This means that you only gather a small amount of a plant and you make sure to leave plenty for local wildlife.

Field garlic, for example, is plentiful in the wintertime. It spreads like kudzu, the infamous invasive of the South, but if you often dig up big bunches of them, you will not see as many next year. I like to cut off the tops, which resemble chives but are smaller, so they will regrow all winter and into early summer.

Native and Invasive Plants

Native plants have been growing in a specific ecosystem for thousands of years. They fit into their surroundings and do not disrupt or crowd out other plants. They help to balance other species of plants and animals. Invasive wild plants are not native to the area they enter and they tend to take over to such an extent that they threaten the local ecosystem. Garlic mustard, for instance, will take over as the predominant ground cover in forests, crowding out and destroying native plants. Kudzu was introduced in the South to help with soil erosion, and it did help with that, but it also

Sustainable foraging

Here are some important questions you should ask yourself when you forage. Keeping these issues in mind will help you forage in a sustainable way and enjoy nature's bounty for years to come.

→ Will harvesting the edible part of this plant kill it? For example, a chunk of sassafras root will invariably break off from the notoriously long taproot when you dig it up; that is the way it regrows. But if you pick the leaves of Loomis's mountain mint rather than cutting at the stem, the plant will die.

→ How much of the plant grows in a particular patch? Is there a lot or just a little? Never take a plant where there are only a few. Let it keep growing, so it will propagate.

→ Is what you are about to harvest eaten by wildlife? Do they have plenty of food in the area appropriate to the season?

→ Is the plant invasive? Invasive plants such as garlic mustard crowd out the existing native flora. You are doing the local ecosystem a favor by harvesting garlic mustard!

The small, whorled leaves of cleavers

grew like wildfire, suppressing and killing native plants.

Invasive plants are also incredibly hard to get rid of. When you forage for an invasive plant, you are helping out the local environment. Please take as much of the plant as you can, and the neighboring plants will thank you for it.

Where to Forage

You might think that you can forage only in the countryside. But many wild edible plants grow in urban areas. In fact, hackberry, which bears fruit with a crunchy, tasty, M&M-like shell, grows only in urban areas.

I live in the city, and when I forage in town, I ask myself two questions:

Is it legal to harvest the plant?
Is the plant growing in a polluted area?

Green areas and public parks are governed by various laws. Some may limit the number of a certain fruit you can gather, some may have no rules at all, and some may prohibit gathering anything within their boundaries. It is best to check at the park's information booth or on the park's Internet website.

Pollution is a constant issue when foraging. When foraging in the city, you need to be extremely cautious about harvesting from vacant lots where the soil could be contaminated with heavy metals and animal waste. Certain plants, like field garlic, pull toxins from the soil. Use caution when harvesting these in an urban setting or close to a road.

One of the best things to forage in the city is fruit. Fruit trees are often planted for their ornamental value in parks, along sidewalks, and in landscaping around houses. Many homeowners neglect the fruit that falls from fruit trees and are annoyed at the tree for creating such a mess. They might be more than happy to let you collect the fruit, but be sure to ask permission first.

In the country, there are two main areas of concern. Never harvest plants by the roadside. They can become polluted from runoff from motor vehicles and trash that gets in the soil. And dogs often foul roadside areas. In addition, beware of harvesting plants from creeks that may have drained through upstream livestock pastures. Watercress, for example, is a highly prized wild edible that grows in spring-fed creeks. More often than not, these creeks are polluted from farm animals with amoeba that can make you very sick.

Nut trees in the countryside, like black walnut, can often be foraged. Black walnut trees are considered by some as a nuisance and even dangerous by people who have an old tree in their yard. If you are out in the country, make sure to get permission from the property owner before walking their land and foraging.

Foraging safely

When foraging, follow these basic safety rules:

→ Always be 100 percent sure of the plant identification.

→ If you've never eaten a particular wild food before, try just a small portion at first to make sure that it agrees with you.

→ Do not harvest right by the side of a heavily trafficked street or highway, to avoid pollution.

→ Find out if the foraging grounds you are considering are sprayed with pesticides or other chemicals, or are near grounds that are chemically treated. Conventionally farmed lands are just as suspect as suburban lawns when it comes to toxic chemical use.

→ If you're going to cultivate a new-to-you city backyard, or you are starting a community garden in which the weeds as well as the planted veggies will be crops, first have the soil tested for lead and other heavy metals.

Foraging Gear

The most important part of a forager's gear is shoes. I highly recommend using comfortable, closed-toed boots. Long pants are essential because you never know when you might have to walk through tall, brushy areas to reach a persimmon tree. I find long pants save my legs from blackberry briars and bugs. Here in the South, bug repellent is a must as well. And a hat: during cooler months, a warm, woolen hat is necessary, and during the warmer months, a ventilated, baseball cap is crucial.

You should carry two other essentials when foraging. A good knife is important for cutting things, and in a pinch, I can use it to dig up something. I also carry a small backpack. I stuff a bag in my back pocket, and I take a foraging pail with a handle. A digging shovel or a tarp can come in handy, too.

Essential Botanical Information for the Forager

When identifying a plant correctly, you use several key characteristics: the shape of the leaves, the way the leaves are arranged, and the roots. Here are the main features to consider:

Leaf Shape

Elliptical An elliptical leaf is broadest at the middle and narrower at the two equal ends.

Lanceolate This lance-shaped leaf is widest at the base and tapers to a long point.

Lobed This leaf has many rounded projections along the edge.

Oval This egg-shaped leaf is longer than it is wide, and wider at the base.

Pinnately compound This leaf is feather-like, with leaflets that grow in two rows opposite each other on a central stalk.

Leaf Arrangement

Opposite Pairs of leaves grow from the same point on a stalk and across from each other.

Alternate Leaves grow from opposite sides at different intervals along the length of the stalk.

Whorled Three or more leaves attach at the same point on the stem, sometimes forming a circle of leaves around a stem node (the place where the leaves or branches originate).

Rosette Leaves that grow in a circle from the same point, which is usually at the soil level, from a taproot.

Roots

Rhizome An underground, horizontal stem that sends out roots at different nodes along it.

Corm The solid, round, enlarged, underground base of a stem that is bulblike.

Taproot A single root that grows straight down into the soil.

In addition to these plant features, when foraging, you'll find leaf edges of different configurations: smooth, toothed, serrated,

The stems of angelica can be candied and used in desserts and cocktails.

and others. You'll also find that flowers on different plants are grouped in different inflorescences: racemes (an unbranched, elongated grouping of blooms that mature from the bottom upward), panicles (a branched grouping of flowers in racemes), catkins (a grouping in a spike or raceme of flowers without petals that are unisexual), and umbels (umbrella-shaped grouping of flowers).

Some Tips for Preparing and Preserving Wild Edibles

Preparing wild foods for a meal and preserving them for another season are your rewards after a day of harvesting. It is heavenly to taste those American hazelnuts chopped and sprinkled over a dish of freshly gathered steamed stinging nettles that evening. And it's comforting to be able to pull out a jar of summer's wild blackberry jam or honeysuckle syrup to have for breakfast in the dead of winter.

Here are some tried-and-true techniques for preparing and preserving your wild harvest:

Winnowing Seeds and Grain

Winnowing is the process of separating the seeds from the chaff, the dry, inedible casing around an edible seed. The most basic form of winnowing is to slowly pour the seeds, with loose chaff attached, from one bowl to the other, and let a breeze blow the chaff off and away from the bowl. If it is windy where you live, you can do this outside. If not, I suggest doing this indoors in front of a fan with a steady draft.

When winnowing a small grain like common amaranth, you will find that some of the chaff will remain attached to the seed. Rub the chaff off these grains with your hands. Also, bigger grains such as wild rice are easier to winnow than smaller ones, because the seed is heavier so it tends to fall directly into the bowl.

Tapping Trees for Sap

Tapping a birch tree for syrup is similar to tapping a maple tree. Start tapping in late winter when the weather is warming and the sap starts to rise in the trees but the leaves have not yet appeared on the trees. Tapping trees correctly does not harm the tree. Only tap trees that have a diameter of more than 10 inches. For a birch tree of 10 to 20 inches diameter, drill only one hole. With bigger trees, you can drill two or sometimes three holes, but no more.

Start by drilling at an upward angle with a $7/16$- or $5/16$-inch drill bit that has been sterilized, and go no more than 2 inches deep. Drill this hole high enough to get a bucket underneath. Insert a spile into the hole: a spile is a metal peg that allows sap to flow out of the tree. (You can also insert a length of food-grade sterile plastic tubing.) Once inserted, lightly tap the spile with a rock or a knife and you should start to see sap flowing. When the spile is in place and the sap is dripping, attach a hook to the spile and hang a lightweight bucket for the sap to flow into, or if using plastic tubing, place the bucket on the ground.

Birch sap does not stay fresh for very long. Keep it in the refrigerator for up to one week. The quicker you boil it down the better. Boiling down the sap is essential for preserving the sap and making it palatable. Boiling evaporates the water in the sap and causes the liquid to reduce down into a syrup. Use the largest pot you have and pour in the sap. Have at least 1 inch of sap in the pot. Lots of steam will come off the sap as it boils, so this step is usually done outside. Boil the sap until it reaches 220°F on a candy thermometer and when the sap cools it has a syrupy consistency. If you do not have a candy thermometer, dip a spoon into the syrup, and if the syrup clings to the spoon, it is ready. Once the sap has boiled down into syrup, pour it into an airtight container like a clean jar and refrigerate for up to three months. If you want to store it longer, preserve it by canning.

Preserving Food by Drying

Drying is one of the oldest methods for preserving foods, and dried foods need little storage space. Sumac fruit can be dried and then ground into a spice, New Jersey tea leaves can be dried and used for tea, and wild blueberries can be dehydrated for later use. The easiest and most basic way to dry edibles is to hang them upside down in a dry, well-ventilated, pest-free spot till they become completely dry. Another is to use an oven or dehydrator to slowly dry the food at low temperature; this works particularly well for fruit.

Preserving Food by Canning

Canning is an important, safe method for preserving food. The canning process involves placing foods in sterilized lidded jars and heating them in a water bath to a temperature that destroys microorganisms that cause food to spoil. During this heating process, air is driven out of the jar, and as the contents cool, a vacuum seal is formed. The vacuum seal prevents air from getting into the product, bringing with it contaminating microorganisms. Making infused syrups, jams, canned fruit, and kimchi (a traditional Korean fermented vegetable dish that is highly nutritious) are excellent ways to preserve your wild harvest.

Infusing Liquids

When you make tea, you just make an infusion by pouring hot water over the tea leaves and letting it steep. Infusing a liquid with a particular plant part is a great way to impart a specific flavor into a liquid. Often times, the edible fragrant flowers of wild edibles do not taste like anything, and the best way to capture their fragrance is by infusing them into a syrup or another liquid. You can make an infusion cold or hot. With cold infusions, it can take six months for the plant part to infuse into the liquid. You also need to shake the bottle once a week or every month. Hot infusions can be made right away, just by pouring a hot liquid over the item and letting it steep. In another type of hot infusion, you simmer the item in a liquid. I have found this technique is the best way to make pine needle tea, for example. I bring water up to a boil and put the green pine needles in and turn the heat down to a simmer. I simmer the pine needles covered for ten to twenty minutes and then serve hot or cold.

Wild Harvests
Season by Season

There is nothing more seasonal than wild edible plants. Wild strawberries are only around for about two weeks, while Loomis's mountain mint can be gathered all summer. I've provided the following guide so that you can know what is in season, when and where, in the Southeast.

The weather is something to keep in mind when using the seasonal guide. It changes from year to year and from state to state, particularly in the Southeast. March weather in Kentucky is different from March weather in Alabama.

In the lists in this seasonal guide, I have indicated a specific plant part, such as daylily shoots, when the plant has more than one edible part or when that plant part is the only edible part of the plant. Where I have listed the plant's name but not a specific part, the whole plant may be edible, but check the individual plant profiles for guidance and further details on how to collect, prepare, and eat each plant part.

Spring

Spring in the South can come and go quickly or slowly, but whether the season is brief or long, it has an early phase and a late part. In early spring, perennial leafy plants like wild lettuce are at their peak. This is also an excellent time to look for asparaguslike pokeweed shoots. The temperatures of mid- to late spring fluctuate wildly depending on the weather that year. Edible blooms like those of redbud, for example, can stay around for quite a while or quickly fade. Be sure to keep watch for the edibles you are interested in harvesting, because the weather can change quickly overnight.

Black locust

Which Plant Where in Early Spring

Open Meadows, Disturbed Soils, Sunny Areas, and the Edges of Sunny Areas

asparagus shoots
basswood leaves
black mustard greens
burdock root
cat's ear dandelion greens
cattail shoots, flowers,
   and pollen
chickweed
chicory leaves and roots
common amaranth young
   leaves and stem

curly dock leaves
dandelion leaves, crown,
   and root
daylily shoots
evening primrose leaves
   and root
field garlic
field mustard greens
field thistle roots
henbit
Jerusalem artichoke tubers

juniper berries
plantain leaves
purple dead nettle
redbud blossoms
salsify leaves and roots
sassafras bark and roots
shepherd's purse leaves
stinging nettle
violet leaves and flowers
Virginia pine needles
wild carrot root and leaves

Woodlands and Partially Shaded Places

basswood leaves
beech leaves
black birch inner bark
   and twigs
chickweed
cleavers stalks and young
   leaves
cow parsnip stem, leafstalks,
   and flowers
crinkleroot roots

daylily shoots
false Solomon's seal shoots
field garlic
garlic mustard leaves and
   roots
greenbrier tips and roots
Japanese knotweed shoots
ramps
redbud blossoms
sassafras bark and roots

Solomon's seal shoots
spicebush twigs
violet leaves and flowers
Virginia pine needles
wild ginger
wintergreen leaves
wood nettle
yellow trout lily

Seashore and Coastal Areas

glasswort stems and leaves
juniper berries
pennywort stems and leaves

red bay leaves
saltwort leaves

sea purslane leaves
   and stems
sea rocket leaves

Wetlands, Riverbanks, Lakesides, Bogs

cattail shoots
cow parsnip stem, leafstalks,
   and flowers

marsh marigold leaves, stalk,
   and flower buds
wapato

watercress stems
   and leaves

Which Plant Where in Mid-Spring to Late Spring

Open Meadows, Disturbed Soils, Sunny Areas, and the Edges of Sunny Areas

Asiatic dayflower
asparagus shoots
basswood blossoms
black locust flowers
black mustard
black nightshade
burdock root and immature
  flower stalks
cat's ear dandelion leaves,
  stems, and flowers
chickweed
chicory roots
common amaranth greens
common mallow leaves
crabapple flowers
curly dock flower stalks
dandelion flowers and root
daylily buds

elderberry flowers
evening primrose leaves
field mustard
field thistle shoots
greenbrier tips and roots
honeysuckle flowers
juneberry fruit
juniper berries
kudzu leaves
lady's thumb
lamb's quarters greens
milkweed florets
mulberry berries
pineapple weed
plantain young leaves
pokeweed shoots
prickly pear pads
purslane

red clover blossoms
salsify shoots
sassafras leaves, bark, and
  roots
sheep sorrel
shepherd's purse shoots
shiso
sow thistle leaves and shoots
spiderwort
stinging nettle
white clover blossoms
wild carrot leaves and roots
wild grape leaves
wild lettuce
wild onion
wisteria flowers
wood sorrel
yarrow leaves

Woodlands and Partially Shaded Places

angelica stems
basswood blossoms
black nightshade
chickweed
cow parsnip stem, leafstalks,
  and flowers
crinkleroot
elderberry flowers

garlic mustard greens,
  flowers, and immature
  seedpods
greenbrier tips and roots
honeysuckle flowers
juneberry berries
kudzu leaves
sassafras leaves, bark,

  and roots
spicebush leaves
violet young leaves
Virginia pine needles
wild ginger
wintergreen leaves
wisteria flowers
wood sorrel

Seashore and Coastal Areas

glasswort
honeysuckle flowers
juniper berries

pennywort stems and leaves
red bay leaves
saltwort leaves

sea purslane leaves and
  stems
sea rocket leaves

Wetlands, Riverbanks, Lakesides, Bogs

angelica stems
cattail
cow parsnip stem, leafstalk,

  leaves, and flowers
mayhaw fruit
pickerelweed leaves

wapato leaves and leafstalks
watercress stems, leaves, and
  flowers

Summer

Summer in the South is really all about fruit. In early to midsummer, a bounty of wild fruits is available for foraging, such as blackberries, raspberries, wineberries, and strawberries. There are other fruits in late summer, such as pawpaw, muscadine (wild grape), and maypop. In addition to fruits in the heat of summer, you'll find many leafy greens thriving, such as lemony wood sorrel, menthol-like Loomis's mountain mint, and earthy shiso. There are also unique plant parts ready for gathering, including sweet oxeye daisy leaves, tangy sumac fruit clusters, and root beer–like sassafras roots.

Which Summer Plant Where

Open Meadows, Disturbed Soils, Sunny Areas, and the Edges of Sunny Areas

Asiatic dayflower

blackberry fruit

black cherry fruit

black locust seedpods

black mustard flowers, seedpods, and seeds

black nightshade berries

blueberry fruit

burdock root and stalk

butternut

chicory flowers

chokeberry fruit

common amaranth leaves

common mallow leaves, flowers, and seeds

dandelion root

daylily flowers and flower pods

elderberry fruit

evening primrose flower buds and flowers

field mustard flowers, seedpods, and seeds

field thistle roots

goldenrod leaves

gooseberry fruit

greenbrier tips and roots

hawthorn fruit

honeysuckle flowers

juniper berries

kudzu flowers

lady's thumb leaves

lamb's quarters greens

Loomis's mountain mint

maypop fruit

milkweed florets and pods

mulberry fruit

New Jersey tea leaves

oxeye daisy leaves

pawpaw fruit

pineapple weed

plantain seeds

purslane leaves and stem

red clover flowers

rose leaves and flowers

salsify flower buds

sassafras leaves, roots, and bark

sheep sorrel

shepherd's purse

shiso

spiderwort

sumac fruit

white clover flowers

wild carrot flowers and seeds

wild grape leaves and fruit

wild plum fruit

wild rice

wild strawberry fruit

wineberry fruit

wood sorrel

yarrow leaves

Woodlands and Partially Shaded Places

angelica seeds
Asiatic dayflower
basswood seeds
blackberry fruit
black birch twigs and bark
black cherry fruit
black nightshade
blueberry fruit
chickweed
cow parsnip stem, leafstalks, and seeds

crinkleroot roots
elderberry fruit
false Solomon's seal fruit
garlic mustard seeds
greenbrier tips and roots
hawthorn fruit
honeysuckle flowers
kudzu flowers
Loomis's mountain mint
mayapple fruit
mayhaw fruit

pawpaw fruit
sassafras leaves, bark, and roots
spicebush leaves and twigs
wild ginger
wild grape leaves
wineberry fruit
wintergreen leaves and fruit
wood sorrel
yellow trout lily bulbs

Seashore and Coastal Areas

beach plum fruit
glasswort stems
juniper berries

pennywort stems
red bay leaves
saltwort leaves

sea purslane leaves and stems

Wetlands, Riverbanks, Lakesides, Bogs

American lotus tubers and seeds
angelica seeds
black birch inner bark

cattail flowers and pollen
chokeberry fruit
cow parsnip stem, leafstalks, and seeds

pickerelweed leaves
wapato leaves, leafstalks, and flower stalks
watercress flowers

Honeysuckle

Fall

Fall can often get a late start down here in the South. The weather fluctuates wildly just like in the spring, and you can often have a few late summer stragglers such as smooth sumac still around in early November. Once fall gets going, the stars of the season are the nuts, like black walnut and acorns from oak trees. Tender, leafy greens such as wild lettuce and chickweed return, and Virginia pine needles appear in a big way as their fragrance deepens and becomes more aromatic. But, there is one thing that sums up the flavor of fall and that is the wild American persimmon. Nothing else has the sweet, datelike, jammy pulp.

Persimmon

Which Autumn Plant Where

Open Meadows, Disturbed Soils, Sunny Areas, and the Edges of Sunny Areas

American hazelnut nuts
American persimmon fruit
apple fruit
Asiatic dayflower
autumn olive berries
basswood fruit
beech nuts
black mustard
black nightshade fruit
black walnut nuts
burdock root
butternut nuts
chickweed
chicory roots and leaves
common amaranth seeds
common mallow leaves,

flowers, and seeds
crabapple fruit
curly dock seeds
dandelion root
daylily corms
evening primrose seeds
field garlic
field mustard
field thistle roots
ginkgo fruit
goldenrod leaves and flowers
hackberry fruit
hawthorn fruit
hickory nuts and bark
Jerusalem artichoke tubers
juniper berries

kousa dogwood fruit
lady's thumb leaves
lamb's quarters seeds
oak acorns
prickly pear fruit and seeds
rose hips
salsify roots
sassafras bark and roots
Virginia pine needles
watercress leaves and stems
white clover blossoms
wild carrot leaves and roots
wild grape fruit
wild pear fruit
yarrow leaves

Woodlands and Partially Shaded Places

American hazelnut berries
American persimmon fruit
beech nuts
black birch inner bark and
    twigs
black nightshade
black walnut nuts
butternut
chickweed

chokeberry fruit
cow parsnip seeds
crinkleroot roots
field garlic
garlic mustard roots and
    leaves
hackberry fruit
hawthorn fruit
sassafras bark and roots

spicebush berries and twigs
Virginia pine needles
wild ginger
wild grape fruit
wild pear fruit
wintergreen leaves and
    berries
yellow trout lily bulbs

Seashore and Coastal Areas

juniper berries
pennywort stems and flowers
red bay leaves

saltwort leaves
sea purslane leaves and
    stems

sea rocket leaves

Wetlands, Riverbanks, Lakesides, Bogs

American lotus tubers
black birch inner bark and
    twigs

cow parsnip seeds
pickerelweed seeds
wapato

watercress

Winter

In the South the coldest weeks of winter are in January and February. Even during the bleakest weeks of the year, there are many wild edible plants that the weather does not damage. Field garlic is around all winter and can be used just like chives or green onions. Chickweed tastes amazing on a cold, bleak day with its vibrant, raw green pea flavor.

Juniper

Which Winter Plant Where

Open Meadows, Disturbed Soils, Sunny Areas, and the Edges of Sunny Areas

black birch inner bark, twigs, sap

chickweed

field garlic

hickory bark

hoary bittercress leaves and flowers

sassafras bark and roots

spicebush twigs

Virginia pine needles

wintergreen leaves and berries

Woodlands and Partially Shaded Places

black birch inner bark, twigs, sap

chickweed

field garlic

hickory bark

sassafras bark and roots

spicebush twigs

Virginia pine needles

wintergreen leaves and berries

Seashore and Coastal Areas

juniper berries

Wetlands, Riverbanks, Lakesides, Bogs

American lotus tubers

black birch inner bark, twigs, sap

marsh marigold leaves, stalk, and flower buds

wapato

watercress leaves and stems

Wild Edible Plants of the Southeast

In western North Carolina, when you face northeast, you see this view over the Appalachian Mountains.

American hazelnut

Corylus americana
filbert

EDIBLE nuts

If you have only eaten store-bought hazelnuts, you will be in for quite a surprise when you try fresh ones. The sweet, earthy flavor of wild hazelnuts is unmistakable.

How to Identify

Hazelnut is a medium to large shrub that forms dense thickets. The stems grow clumped together at the base of the shrub. There can be anywhere from six to forty stems per clump. They grow crooked and tend to lean. The leaves are alternate, roughly toothed, and oval, growing 2 to 5 inches long. The male flowers are borne in catkins and the female flowers are tiny

Delicious hazelnuts grow in the wild, hiding in plain sight.

and hard to notice. The nuts ripen in late summer and grow in tight clusters of up to fifteen at the tips of branches. The nuts are hard-shelled, smooth, and light brown when ripe. Each nut is wrapped in a pair of ruffled leaves with sticky, gland-tipped hairs that hide and protect it.

Another hazelnut bush in our region, beaked hazelnut (*Corylus cornuta*), looks just like American hazelnut except that the nuts look different. Instead of two ruffled leaves wrapped around the nut, there is a tapering tube or "beak" with tiny spines.

Where and When to Gather

American hazelnut grows in the understory of young, open forests, along fences, at the edge of woods, and in old fields. The husk will still be green when the nuts are ripe. Ripe hazelnuts should be light brown. If you wait until the husks are brown, the nuts will all be gone. Gather hazelnuts in late August and early September.

How to Gather

Gather hazelnuts by pulling the entire cluster from the bush. The best way to shell the nuts is by storing them in a dry, squirrel-proof place for a week until the husk turns brown. Then the nuts are easier to remove from the husks. Once the nuts have been removed, you still need to crack the shells to get at the nutmeats. Hazelnuts are easier to shell than other wild nuts.

How to Eat

Hazelnuts are delicious in savory and sweet dishes. One of my favorite ways to use hazelnuts is with pears because the flavors are heavenly complements. Together, they also make a tasty salad vinaigrette. Chopped hazelnuts and maple syrup are incredible on homemade vanilla ice cream.

How to Preserve

Hazelnuts store well in the shell without refrigeration in a cool, dry place. They store really well in any kind of container with or without a lid. If you store them in a cabinet, be sure your container is rodent proof. They also keep well in the freezer in ziplock freezer bags.

Future Harvests

There is no need to limit your harvest.

American lotus

Nelumbo lutea

water chinkapin

EDIBLE young leaves, tubers, seeds

American lotus lives in freshwater ponds, lakes, and sloughs. It has large, round leaves, and its beautiful white blossoms are North America's largest native flower. The seeds have a caramel-like flavor and the roots are sweet and starchy.

How to Identify

American lotus is an aquatic perennial, growing up to 3 feet above the water, with round, cup-shaped or flat leaves up to 24 inches across that grow from a stiff, rough, 1-inch-thick stalk. The stalk extends from rhizomes growing in the muddy bottom of the water. At the end of the rhizomes, a light cream-yellow tuber grows 3 to 14 inches long. Lotus flowers are fragrant, creamy yellow, and have many petals up to 10 inches wide. They open in the morning and close at night.

Water lily looks similar, but the leaves have a slit in them. I advise not eating water lily. Chinese lotus, *Nelumbo*

The nuts (or seeds) of American lotus grow in the seed head.

American lotus has round, slightly concave leaves.

nucifera, looks very similar to American lotus, but the flowers are a light red and the seeds are longer. Chinese lotus is not native to America but has escaped into the wild in the South. It is edible and can be used in the same way as American lotus.

Where and When to Gather

The young lotus leaves should be gathered between April and June when the sides of the leaf are still rolled up. Tubers growing in shallow water ripen in mid-August, while those that grow in deeper water ripen in September or sometimes early October. The seeds ripen from September to October, depending on water depth and weather.

How to Gather

Gather the young lotus leaves by breaking or pinching them off with your hands.

The tubers are fun to gather: you will get muddy and wet. First, use your hands to follow the stem of the plant down into the mud, where it connects to a rhizome. The rhizomes grow horizontally in both directions. You will need to pick which direction to follow. Usually there is a rhizome that is smaller than the one on the other side of the stem. Follow the smaller rhizome to the end, where it will expand into a tuber. Gently loosen the mud around the tuber and pull backward, not straight up. Tubers often grown as doubles, and by gathering them this way you run little risk of one breaking off.

The seed head can be easily broken off by hand, whether you are wading in the water or standing on dry ground. But the best way to gather seed heads is by canoe with two people. One person can paddle among the plants and the other can collect the seed heads. You can fill a canoe up pretty fast this way. Once you have gathered the seed heads, you need to remove the seeds, which should be large and plump, filling the cavities in the seed head. When first ripe, the receptacles will be soft and green. At this stage, you can use your hands to remove the nuts or just crack open the seed head. After ripening, the seed head turns brown, dries out, and shrinks. Once dry, the seeds store indefinitely. Crack open a dried seed like you would a black walnut or hickory nut.

How to Eat

The leaves once cooked can be used to wrap cooked rice, meat, fish, and vegetables. You can use the leaves like you would a tamale wrapper or banana leaf.

The tubers are the most commonly used part of the plant. You can find these at Asian markets, but the ones you pull up yourself will be much fresher. The tubers must be peeled with a vegetable peeler before using. After peeling the thin skin, cut off the ends and look to see if the insides are clean. If not, run water through the hollow channels that run from end to end. Cut the tuber crosswise into slices, which are very beautiful, with their symmetrical holes. When the tubers are young, they have a crisp texture, translucent flesh, and a mild, sweet flavor that is delicious raw, pickled, candied, or battered and fried. The tubers can also be roasted, boiled, baked, or stir-fried with other vegetables. Older tubers get very starchy and are not as sweet. But you can extract the starch from them.

Lotus has a long history of culinary use in Asia, and Native Americans traditionally cultivated it. The seeds, before they dry, are soft, chewy, and taste similar to a chestnut. That is why the plant is also called water chinkapin. Once the seeds are dry, they take on a caramel-like flavor. At this stage, they are often candied or used in desserts. The dried seeds are turned into a paste to fill traditional moon cakes made for the Chinese mid-autumn festival in October.

How to Preserve

Keep the leaves in an airtight container with a damp paper towel on top of them. If you are using the young, green seeds, use them as soon as possible because they do not hold up well. The dried seeds can be stored indefinitely in a dark, dry place. Keep the tubers in an airtight container in a refrigerator for up to six weeks. The tubers can also be sliced and dried in a dehydrator for use in the winter.

Future Harvests

There is no need to limit your harvest of the seeds. But if you are gathering the tubers, only gather from well-established, plentiful stands of American lotus.

American lotus tubers grow at the end of the rhizomes.

American persimmon

Diospyros virginiana

possumwood

`EDIBLE` fruit

The American persimmon tree, which is native to the United States, produces fruit in the late summer with a jellylike texture and a sweet, datelike flavor that is irresistible.

How to Identify

The American persimmon tree grows 15 to 100 feet tall and has thick, grayish black, scaly bark. The oval leaves are alternate, toothless, and grow up to 6 inches long and 3 inches wide. The pale yellow female flowers are bell-shaped with four petals and eight stamens. The smaller male flower produces pollen but no fruit. The fruit is globular, orange, and 1 to 1½ inches wide.

Where and When to Gather

American persimmon grows in many different areas: the understory of forests, in full sun, and along roads. Start looking for ripe persimmons in late August. It is a myth that persimmons do not ripen until after frost, but it is true that they do become sweeter from frost. The fruit ripens as the days get shorter. The best fruit can be found in October through November.

These persimmons are ripe and ready to eat.

The bark of the persimmon tree looks similar to dogwood bark.

How to Gather

Gather ripe persimmons by picking them up off the ground or by shaking the tree. Ripe persimmons are very soft. When they are underripe, they have an astringent, slightly bitter taste.

How to Eat

The flavor of a ripe persimmon is heavenly on a cold day in the fall. It's hard to define the flavor: it's sort of like a soft, ripe date. The texture is like jam, and the sweetness complements fatty, rich meats like duck. Persimmons are tasty in breads, puddings, and desserts.

How to Preserve

Keep persimmons in an airtight container in the refrigerator. Unripe persimmons can be placed in a paper bag with unwaxed apples to help ripen them.

Future Harvests

You can gather as many persimmons as you want.

angelica

Angelica species

EDIBLE young leaves, young stem, green seeds

Angelica has long been eaten in Europe for the unique flavor of its leaves and stems, a mix of juniper, celery, and asparagus.

How to Identify

Two types of angelica grow in the Southeast. Mountain angelica (*Angelica triquinta*) is a perennial that grows up to 5 feet tall and has a smooth, thick, reddish stem. The green, coarsely toothed, three-part leaves have sheaths that enclose the leafstalk at the base. Mountain angelica starts to flower in July, producing tiny, greenish white, five-petaled flowers that grow in an umbrella shape 3 to 6 inches wide. Flattened, green seeds form in August to September.

Purplestem angelica (*Angelica atropurpurea*) is a biennial that grows 4 to 9 feet tall at lower elevations and has a smooth, dark purple stem, with leaves that are like those of mountain angelica. It starts to flower in June, producing tiny, greenish white, five-petaled flowers that form a globular shape. The flattened, green seeds form in July to September.

Where and When to Gather

Look for purplestem angelica in swamps and along streambeds or for mountain angelica in the high mountains in woods or in open, rocky areas. Gather the young stem from April to May before the plant starts to bloom, and harvest the leaves at the same time. Gather the seeds while they are still green from June to September.

How to Gather

Use a pair of shears or a sharp knife to gather the young stem or leaves. The green seeds can be gathered by using your hand to pinch off a flower cluster. Whether you are gathering the young stems, young leaves, or greens seeds, have some sort of container or bag to put them in.

How to Eat

Angelica traditionally is eaten by candying the stems or the leafstalks. If you candy the stems, make sure to peel them to remove the bitter skin. After candying, the stems can be used like you would candied citrus peel in desserts and mixed drinks. Besides candying, you can braise the stems in

Angelica has large elliptical leaves and a celerylike stem.

soups and stews. I do not recommend eating angelica raw. Use the leaves to season things like you would a bay leaf. The seeds can be used like caraway or celery seed. Angelica seeds were used traditionally to flavor gin and vermouth.

How to Preserve

Candy the stems and store in an airtight container. The seeds should be stored in an airtight container in the refrigerator for a couple of weeks. They do not last long because their aromatic oil dissipates over time. They are best used within a couple of weeks. Try making some gin or vermouth, or use them as a pickling spice.

Future Harvests

Harvest angelica sparingly because the plants usually do not grow in great numbers.

Warning

Angelica looks similar to two deadly poisonous plants in the same family, water hemlock (*Cicuta maculata*) and poison hemlock (*Conium maculatum*). Neither one has swollen sheaths that form at the base of the leafstalk and wrap around the leaf like those of angelica do. Be very careful when foraging for angelica!

apple
Malus species
`EDIBLE` fruit

Apples growing wild have a deeper, more assertive sweet-to-tart apple flavor than cultivated apples.

How to Identify

Wild apple trees grow up to 30 feet tall but are often smaller. They have scaly gray bark and alternate leaves that are 2 to 4 inches long, oval, pointed, and have small teeth on the margins. They have a faint fuzziness on their undersides. The fragrant pink or white flowers have five petals and are less than 1½ inches in diameter.

Wild apples look much like the ones you buy at the store, but they are smaller. Remember that the fruit has grown all by itself, with no spraying or other care, so the apples may have scabs, wormholes, or fire rust, which you can just cut out. The size can vary greatly, as can the color, which may be green, red, yellow, or somewhere in between.

Where and When to Gather

Typically, apples start to ripen in the Southeast in August and the season goes to October.

How to Gather

Pluck apples from the tree using your hands, and have at least one bucket to put them in. If you find a tree loaded with fruit, you can also use a fruit picker, which is a long, wooden pole with a small metal basket at the end that allows you to pick high fruit you cannot reach. Often there is lots of fruit on the ground around the tree, but those apples can be bruised or smashed, so inspect the fruit for damage or insects before using.

How to Eat

My favorite way to eat an apple is fresh out my hand, and it is a good way to see if the fruit is sweet, tart, or sour. Apples that are sweet help balance the bitterness of endive in a salad; apples that are tart make excellent baked items like pies. Tart or sour apples can also be used to make an apple-cabbage slaw that pairs well with pork. The bruised apples you find on the ground can be perfect for making fermented products.

This wild apple tree grows on the side of a hill in the mountains.

How to Preserve

Apples should be stored in a root cellar or crisper drawer in the refrigerator to preserve their freshness. Apple butter is a delicious way to preserve sweet apples. Tart apples can be made into vinegar, jelly, and cider.

Future Harvests

There is no need to limit your harvest of apples.

Asiatic dayflower

Commelina communis

dayflower

EDIBLE flower, leaves, stem, seeds

The beautiful, mildly sweet blossoms of Asiatic dayflower can be used as a garnish and are delicious when candied.

How to Identify

Asiatic dayflower blooms have two blue petals above and one tiny white petal below. Each flower stays open for only one day. The lance-shaped leaves have smooth margins, are 1 to 4 inches long and ½ to 1½ inches wide, and have parallel veins. The leaf base clasps the stems, and there are often hairs where they connect. The individual, round stem grows up to

Asiatic dayflower has striking small blue and white flowers.

2½ feet long, sprawls in a loose combination of upright and horizontal growth, and stays juicy and tender throughout the summer. The stem is slightly swollen at the nodes where the leaves join it, and will root if it comes into contact with moist soil, which is how the plants spread. The tiny, green seeds look like green peas.

Where and When to Gather
Asiatic dayflower likes damp or disturbed soil and partial shade. It is common in gardens, parks, sidewalks, and shady yards. It is in season throughout the summer and into the early fall.

How to Gather
Gather Asiatic dayflower by snapping it off with your fingers, or use scissors to cut several inches of the stem, flowers, leaves, and all. The flowers should be gathered early in the morning or late in the evening, not in the heat of the day, to hold up well. The seeds are in the heart-shaped pods. Use your fingers to break open the pod to remove the seed.

How to Eat
I love the sweet, mild flavor of the leaves and stem raw in a salad. If you cook them, stir-fry them quickly or add them at the end of the cooking process. The green pea-like seeds taste similar to the leaves and stem. It is hard to collect enough to use, so they are best as a snack. The striking blue and white flowers make stunning embellishments on cakes or salads, and they are tasty when candied.

How to Preserve
Store the fresh flowers in an airtight container with a damp paper towel on top in a refrigerator for up to one week.

Future Harvests
Asiatic dayflower is considered a weed that self-seeds prolifically. There is no need to limit your harvest.

asparagus

Asparagus officinalis

EDIBLE shoots

Asparagus loves to escape cultivation into the wild. Look for asparagus near the cultivated variety at the edge of fields, woods, and ditches. The tender, slender spears are a real treat in the early spring.

How to Identify

Asparagus growing in the wild is fleshy, unbranched, and topped with scale-like leaves that are actually bracts. The young shoots, or spears, look just like the cultivated version, but skinnier. Left unharvested, the shoots turn into slim-stalked, branched plants up to 6 feet tall with delicate, feathery foliage that branches out.

Where and When to Gather

In early spring, asparagus pops up from its perennial roots looking pretty much like its cultivated version. It likes to grow in full to partial sun, in moist soil often at the edges of roads, along fences, at the edge of woods, and in drainage ditches. If asparagus is growing in a garden, chances are there is more nearby that has escaped.

The spears of wild asparagus are perfect for harvest in the spring.

This wild asparagus has gone to seed.

I often come across asparagus when it has gone to seed, because it is easier to notice this way. So I make a note of it and come back the following year, earlier in the spring, to harvest the young spears. Wild asparagus also usually grows one spear, instead of a crown like the cultivated version.

How to Gather
Gather asparagus by using a knife to cut the stalk a couple of inches above the ground.

How to Eat
Asparagus growing in the wild tastes just like the cultivated variety you find at farmers' markets, but fresher and sweeter. The slender spears, wild or cultivated, are not tender all the way down each stalk. Usually, the lower section is tough and woody. Hold the asparagus spear in both hands and bend it. It will snap where the tender and woody sections meet. The woody section can be used for vegetable stock. Use tender wild asparagus any way that the cultivated type is used. Cook them lightly: blanch them for no more than a minute, bake them in a frittata, or lightly roast them in a wood-burning oven.

How to Preserve
Asparagus will keep fresher longer in your refrigerator if you place them upright in a container with water in the bottom.

Future Harvests
If you harvest asparagus spears repeatedly from the same plant, eventually you weaken the plant. To harvest sustainably, cut asparagus shoots from a particular patch only once per year and do not take all the spears.

Warning
Female asparagus plants produce small, bright red berries that are poisonous. Do not harvest these.

autumn olive

Elaeagnus umbellata
silverberry, autumnberry

`EDIBLE` berries

Autumn olives are striking, with silver flecks that dot the red berries. The plants' bountiful fruit has a sweet-tart flavor that is a mix of pomegranate, plum, and raspberry.

How to Identify

Autumn olive is a shrub growing 12 to 18 inches tall, with alternate, long, elliptical, leathery 2- to 4-inch-long leaves with a silvery underside. The dull, yellow flowers growing in clusters are produced in April. Each sweetly fragrant flower has four petals. The fruits are about the size of a pea and start out green, then turn bright orange-red when ripe. The berries, leaves, and twigs are marked by small, silvery flakes, which are distinctive.

Another plant sometimes confused with autumn olive is called buffaloberry

The autumn olive shrub has red berries with silver flecks.

(*Shepherdia canadensis*). It has shiny scales like autumn olive, but the scales are brownish rather than silver and the leaves grow in pairs instead of alternately.

Where and When to Gather

Autumn olive is a native of Asia, and was introduced into the United States in 1830 for soil improvement, erosion control, landscaping, and wildlife food. Like many imported exotic plants, it soon became invasive. In some parts of the country, it is considered noxious because of its invasiveness. It is one of the few nonlegume plants that fixes nitrogen in the soil. So, look for it in fields where the soil is poor, on eroded hillsides, and around landscaped buildings.

The best time to gather the berries is in September, and you can still find lots of ripe fruit into mid-October.

How to Gather

Gather autumn olives by holding a bucket underneath a branch and loosening the berries with your other hand so that they fall into the bucket. You could also lay down a dropcloth and loosen the berries so they fall onto it. Try not to crush too many berries when loosening them.

How to Eat

The flavor of autumn olives is a sweet-tart mix of fruity tastes. They are delicious raw. Some people eat the whole berry, seed and pulp. The fruit makes excellent jams, jellies, and sauces. If you are making a sauce or purée, the juice will separate from the solids, because the fruit is high in lycopene, which is not water-soluble. The juice will be clear and is utterly delicious. The red color will stay with the pulp. The pulp makes tasty fruit leather. The fruit makes an excellent vinegar or you can make your own miso.

How to Preserve

The fruit should be stored in an airtight container in the refrigerator. Autumn olives lend themselves really well to fermented products such as vinegar and miso.

Future Harvests

There is no need to limit your harvest of this delicious, invasive plant.

basswood

Tilia americana

linden

`EDIBLE` young leaves, unopened flower buds, flowers, fruit

Basswood is known for the sweet, honeylike fragrance of its blooms, which is detectable from far away.

How to Identify

Basswood is a fast-growing, deciduous, shade-tolerant native tree that grows 60 to 100 feet tall. Younger trees have smooth, thin bark and older trees have bark with long, parallel ridges. Leaves are alternate, simple, and heart-shaped. The flowers are yellowish white, 1/2 inch wide, with five petals that grow in small, drooping clusters. Basswood seeds are small, round, and pea-size.

The flowers of the basswood tree grow in clusters.

Where and When to Gather

Basswood grows in moist, fertile, well-drained forests. Gather young leaves in early April, harvest the small flowers in mid- to late spring, and collect the pealike seeds in early October.

How to Gather

Gather the young leaves and flowers by using scissors to cut them off. The fruits (nuts or seeds) are laborious to shell, but well worth it.

How to Eat

The young leaves are best eaten raw. They have a soft, chewy texture and a pleasant, mild flavor. Use them in salads. The unopened flower buds have an interesting texture when cooked and a mild flavor.

Make sure to remove all the stems from the buds. The flowers can be infused to make a delicious tea. The nuts have a thick shell and taste like sunflower seeds. The nuts can be used in a lot of different ways: roast them to use in dishes, ice cream, or to make miso.

How to Preserve

Keep the young leaves, unopened flower buds, flowers, and nuts in airtight containers in the refrigerator.

Future Harvests

You can gather as many basswood nuts as you want.

beach plum

Prunus maritima

EDIBLE fruit

Beach plums are fantastic because of their sweet pulp, sour skin, and slight saltiness from the sea.

How to Identify

Beach plum is a coastal-area shrub that grows 4 to 8 feet tall. It spreads by root suckers and forms thickets. The bark of young twigs is red-brown, but becomes dark gray on older branches. In early spring, the shrub starts blooming with five-petaled, ½-inch-wide white flowers that have numerous stamens and a single pistil. The shrub begins to leaf out and bloom at the same time. The leaves are oval, finely toothed, alternate, and lighter and fuzzier on the undersides than on the green upper surfaces. The round fruit

Beach plums can be found ripening near the shore.

dangle from short stems, and they look exactly like a cultivated plum except they are much smaller, usually less than 1 inch in diameter. Beach plums start out red and turn blue to dark purple when ripe with a whitish coating called bloom that you can rub off with your finger.

Where and When to Gather
Look for beach plum near the seashore. Collect the fruit in late summer when they turn purple.

How to Gather
Gather beach plums by hand. Make sure to have a bucket or bag with you. A hat will work in a pinch. Be careful not to crush the fruit.

How to Eat
Beach plums are really good eaten out of hand. They also make fantastic wine. Anything you can do with a cultivated plum you can do with a beach plum. Plum upside-down cake is wonderful. People often discard the sour skin, but dried plum halves (with the skin on) make a tasty sweet-and-sour snack. When using plums, remove the inedible pits.

How to Preserve
Store fresh beach plums in an airtight container in the refrigerator. Beach plums make excellent vinegar, jam, jelly, and sauces.

Future Harvests
There is no need to limit your harvest.

beech
Fagus grandifolia

EDIBLE young leaves, nuts

Every two or three years, beech trees produce nuts that are prized for their unique woodsy, nutty flavor.

How to Identify
The beech tree is a magnificent tree found in mixed hardwood forests. The alternate, papery thin to leathery leaves cling to the branches all winter and rattle in the wind. Beech is a slow-growing tree that can become up to 100 feet high and 3 feet wide, with mottled gray bark. The fruit is a yellowish brown nut that is enclosed in a triangular, spiny burr. Beech trees are said to not produce nuts until they are forty years old.

Where and When to Gather
Beech trees commonly grow on slopes in hardwood forests. Nuts ripen in September and October.

How to Gather
Gather the young leaves before they have unfurled. They start to appear between late March and late April, depending on the region of the Southeast. They can be eaten raw. Timing is essential when gathering the nuts, because immature nuts are often

The outer shell of beechnuts has distinctive little hooks.

The beech tree has smooth bark.

Very young beech leaves are edible, ideally before they have unfurled.

knocked to the ground by wind, and animals devour the ripe ones. Bad nuts tend to be hollow and curve inward, while good ones are usually darker and have flat sides.

How to Eat

Beechnuts are laborious to shell. You can break the thin brown shell around the white kernel with your fingernail. Or if you roast them whole, the shell will come off easily. The nuts' woodsy flavor is only enhanced when they are roasted. You can use beechnuts in any way that other nuts are used.

How to Preserve

Beechnuts go rancid quickly. You can refrigerate them for up to a week. To preserve them, dry them or make nut oil.

Future Harvests

There is no need to limit your harvest.

blackberry

Rubus argutus

sawtooth blackberry, Florida blackberry

`EDIBLE` fruit

Picking blackberries as a kid is one of my fondest memories. Nothing beats a sun-ripened, juicy blackberry on a hot, humid summer day.

How to Identify

Blackberries grow on arching woody stems, called canes, up to 10 feet tall. The canes are reddish brown with sharp thorns and three to five leaves that are oval, serrated, and have pointy tips. The flowers are symmetrical, delicate, white, and have five petals. The fruits start out whitish green, turning red and then black when ripe. There are many different species of blackberries—all edible—and they don't all look the same. Some are small, while others are large.

Blackberries turn black, plump, and soft when they are ripe.

Where and When to Gather

Blackberries grow in open fields, clearings, and thickets. The fruit ripens from late June to mid-July in the Southeast. Always taste blackberries before you pick them, because not all have wonderful flavor. In my experience, blackberries in huge thickets that have been growing for many years are the best.

How to Gather

Gather blackberries by pulling the berries individually off the plant. For picking, you will want to wear a long-sleeved shirt and long pants to protect you from the thorns.

How to Eat

Blackberries can be eaten in myriad ways. Fresh over oatmeal is one of my favorites. Besides making jams, jellies, syrup, and all kinds of sweet desserts, they are excellent in savory preparations. For example, think about using blackberries to complement fatty, rich meats like duck or pork. The sweetness of the blackberries balances the richness of the meat. I love to make fruit compote with the berries, but my favorite way of using blackberries in savory dishes is fermenting them into a vinegar.

How to Preserve

Blackberries can be kept fresh in the refrigerator for several days. If you need to freeze them for later use, freeze them laid out on a cookie sheet so they freeze separately and won't stick to each other, then put them in a ziplock bag. Freezing the berries will cause them to turn mushy, which is fine if you plan to make pies, jam, or syrup.

Future Harvests

You will never be able to pick all the blackberries. Harvest as much as you like.

black birch

Betula lenta
sweet birch

EDIBLE inner bark, twigs, sap

Black birches are extremely useful. Their wood makes great furniture, and the bark can be used to craft canoes. The inner bark was once used as paper, and the twigs and inner bark can be used to make tasty infusions. The trees also produce edible sap that can be made into a syrup.

How to Identify

Black birch is a tree 50 to 80 feet tall with dark, smooth bark that looks like it has dark horizontal cracks. Its green leaves are alternate, oval, pointed, and serrated. Male and female flowers grow separately on the same tree. The male flowers are long drooping catkins. The fruits are small, upright cones 1 inch long with tiny seeds.

One way to identify black birch is to scratch the twigs, which releases a wintergreen smell.

The leaf of the black birch tree has parallel veins.

This huge, old black birch has smooth, crackly bark.

Where and When to Gather

Black birch grows in deep, fertile, well-drained soil but is also found growing in drier, rocky soil. The inner bark can be gathered at any time of the year. The twigs can be gathered during the spring and summer. The sap is collected from the trunk of the tree in late winter.

How to Gather

Cut the inner bark only from fallen trees so that you do not injure living trees. Gather the inner bark by cutting away the outer bark. Collect the twigs by cutting them off with pruning shears. Gather the sap by tapping the tree in the same manner as a maple tree.

How to Eat

The edible parts of black birch smell and taste like wintergreen. The inner bark tastes like wintergreen Life Savers. You can use the inner bark to flavor desserts, cocktails, or beer, or grind it into flour. The twigs can be used for infusions or as a tasty trail snack. The sap once cooked down can be used just like maple syrup (see Tapping Trees for Sap, page 18).

How to Preserve

The inner bark and twigs should be kept in an airtight container in the refrigerator. The cooked-down sap can be stored in an airtight container at room temperature.

Future Harvests

Never gather the inner bark from standing, healthy trees. Look for fallen trees or ones that are dying.

black cherry

Prunus serotina

`EDIBLE` fruit

While walking through old, overgrown pastures or fields, you may notice this tree because of its small, edible, dark cherries that have a bittersweet cherry flavor. The wood can be used to smoke meats and seafood. Branches and twigs impart a classic cherry wood aroma when used in the smoking process.

How to Identify

Black cherry is a medium-size tree that grows up to 70 feet tall. Its dark green, glossy leaves are 2 to 6 inches long with tiny hairs on the underside of the midrib. The bark may look smooth, but it is actually somewhat rough with lightly colored reddish brown horizontal stripes. The flowers grow on long racemes with symmetrical five-petaled flowers, which produce small fruits ½ inch wide that turn red and then black when ripe.

Where and When to Gather

Black cherry grows in open fields, old pastures, open woods—just about anywhere.

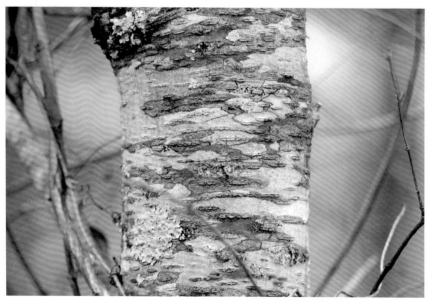

The black cherry tree has smooth, shiny bark with horizontal stripes.

These wild cherries will turn black when ripe.

The best time to gather the fruit is mid-June when the cherries are dark purple, almost black.

How to Gather
Pick black cherries by plucking the ripe fruits off the tree with your hands.

How to Eat
Black cherries have a unique tart-sweet flavor. Some trees produce bigger and better fruit than others, so taste them before collecting. Since the fruit is small and has big pits, make sure to gather a good amount. They can be cooked down into sauce to go with meat or fish. The fruits offer a refreshing flavor for punch.

How to Preserve
Keep black cherries in an airtight container in the refrigerator. They can also be used to make jellies.

Future Harvests
There is no need to limit your harvest because black cherry is a prolific self-seeder.

black locust

Robinia pseudoacacia

EDIBLE flowers, green seeds

Black locust is widely planted as an ornamental tree for its creamy white, sweet-smelling spring flowers. These edible flowers are sweet with a hint of vanilla and produce green seedpods that contain edible green seeds.

The fragrant pealike flowers of black locust bloom in April.

How to Identify

Black locust is native to the Southeast, growing up to 80 feet tall with dark brown-gray, deeply furrowed bark. Its green, compound leaves grow 8 to 14 inches long alternately with many smooth-margined, oval leaflets 2 inches long. The fragrant, pealike flowers are borne loosely, hanging in clusters up to 8 inches long. The later green seedpods are flattened and 3 to 4 inches long. Inside each pod are several small, green seeds that look like tiny butter beans and turn dark brown as the seedpod dries out.

Where and When to Gather

Black locust grows along roadsides, in old fields, in urban areas planted as an ornamental, and in the mountains of the Southeast. The flowers start to bloom in April and usually only last for about a week, so cut them when you see them. Start looking for the green seedpods in June. The seeds inside are edible while still green. Once they start to turn brown, they are too tough to eat.

How to Gather

Gather the flowers by using scissors to cut them off the stem. Have a container by your feet or tie it onto your belt for ease of harvest. The seedpods can be handpicked and placed into a bag or container. Then you need to shell the seedpods, which is similar to shelling fresh peas or beans.

How to Eat

Black locust flowers are very fragrant and have a crunchy texture. I like the flowers best raw as a garnish on desserts. But, they can also be used as an infusion for mixed drinks or added to cream-based sauces. The shelled seeds taste like beans, so use them like you would use lima beans.

How to Preserve

The flowers should be kept with a damp paper towel on top in an airtight container in the refrigerator for up to a week. The seeds should be stored in a ziplock bag in the refrigerator for up to two weeks.

Future Harvests

There is generally no need to limit your harvest because you cannot reach all the flowers or seedpods. But with smaller trees, do not take all the flowers or seedpods.

black mustard

Brassica nigra

EDIBLE flower buds, flowers, leaves, root, seedpods, seeds, stalk

Black mustard is cultivated in huge fields for the seeds, which are used to make yellow mustard. It also self-seeds prolifically in gardens and is often considered an invasive weed.

How to Identify

Black mustard grows a stem up to 3 feet tall from a basal rosette. The smooth, green, pointed leaves that clasp the stem are up to 20 inches long. The leaves at the base of the stem are deeply lobed, and farther up the stem they are teardrop-shaped. Mustard flowers have four yellow petals in a distinctive cross pattern typical of the genus *Brassica*. They grow in clusters, and before the flowers open, the clusters of green flower buds look like broccoli florets. Mustard's slender seedpods have a narrow, pointed tip.

Where and When to Gather

Black mustard loves gardens, fields, and disturbed soil. It starts appearing in

These unopened flower buds and leaves of black mustard are at the perfect stage for gathering.

September and grows until late May. You can gather black mustard at any time. Once established, it self-seeds prolifically.

How to Gather
The whole plant can be eaten: flower buds, flowers, leaves, root, seedpods, seeds, and stalk. Harvest by cutting with scissors or digging up the plant with the root.

How to Eat
I love to eat the flowers and flower buds. They have a sharp, spicy flavor. The flavor of black mustard greens is similar to that of cultivated mustard greens. The flowers are excellent raw as part of a salad or as a garnish. The buds are great pickled, sautéed, or stir-fried. The greens and buds are also excellent in kimchi.

How to Preserve
Keep any part of black mustard with a damp paper towel on top in an airtight container in the refrigerator. Grind the small, black seeds to make your own yellow mustard. Pickle the flower buds and leaves in kimchi.

Future Harvests
There is no need to limit your harvest of this invasive plant.

Brassica

The genus *Brassica* is in the mustard family, Brassicaceae, which includes many cultivated vegetables, such as cabbage, collard greens, broccoli, arugula, kale, mustard greens, radishes, and turnips. There are also several edible brassicas that grow wild. Black mustard and field mustard have a spicy flavor that is similar to, if not more assertive than, that of cultivated vegetables in the mustard family.

Black mustard often comes up in fields and gardens. When foraging, you can identify *Brassica* plants by their characteristic small yellow flowers with four petals in a distinctive cross pattern. The flowers grow in clusters, and before they open, the clusters of green flower buds look like broccoli florets. The slender seedpods have a narrow, pointed tip.

black nightshade

Solanum nigrum

EDIBLE leaves, berries

The first thing that comes to mind when you hear the words "black nightshade" is poison. But there is nothing poisonous about the berries, leaves, or stem of black nightshade, all of which taste like tomatoes. There are toxic nightshade plants, but black nightshade is not one of them.

How to Identify

Black nightshade is a branching plant that can grow up to 3 feet high and 4 feet wide but is often smaller. The leaves grow in an alternate arrangement with a slightly variable leaf shape that is somewhere between an oval and a diamond, with few if any soft teeth on the margins. The leaves are softly hairy, whereas the stems are sometimes hairless. The leafstalks often have thin wings or ridges running down their sides. The ½-inch or smaller, five-petaled white flowers hang in upside-down clusters. The plant blooms almost continuously from

When ripe, the berries of black nightshade are bluish black.

early summer through early fall. Black nightshade's fruit is bluish black when ripe. Each individual berry is a smooth sphere about ¼ inch in diameter with a five-pointed calyx that is smaller than the berry is wide. The fruit does not ripen all at the same time.

There are several plants called black nightshade in the genus *Solanum*. Several so closely resemble *S. nigrum* that they used to all be grouped together under that name.

Where and When to Gather
Black nightshade grows as a weed in disturbed soils in partial shade. The greens are in season from late spring until they flower in early summer. Once the plants flower, the greens become bitter and may contain harmful amounts of solanine, a toxic compound that is common in the nightshade family. Berries begin to ripen in August, and the plants continue to produce fruit into the fall.

How to Gather
Harvest the leaves before the plants flower by using shears to cut the leafstalks. Pick the berries when they are dark purple to black. The unripe, green fruit is not edible. Ripe black nightshade berries grow in bunches and are fragile and squash easily. Use a shallow container to collect them in, so the berries will not be damaged.

How to Eat
Ripe black nightshade fruit is juicy and contains numerous seeds like a tomatillo.

The flavor is like a fruity tomato. The fruit can be used in any way you would use a tomato. The berries can be eaten raw or cooked. Think sauces, like salsa verde. Black nightshade greens must be cooked in boiling water for ten to fifteen minutes. If the greens still taste a bit bitter, boil them a few minutes longer.

How to Preserve
Preserve the harvest by making sauces that you can or freeze.

Future Harvests
Black nightshade is considered an invasive species in some places. It self-seeds well and will propagate itself if there are a few berries left behind on each plant. I would leave some behind.

Warning
There is also a poisonous nightshade, *Atropa belladonna*, which confusingly is also sometimes called black nightshade. Fortunately, it's easy to tell the edible black nightshades from *Atropa belladonna* and other toxic species. Compare the identification features of *Solanum* species with those of the poisonous plant. *Solanum* leaves are wider than they are tall and frequently riddled with holes because bugs munch on them. Poisonous nightshade fruit is borne singly and is bigger, with the five-pointed calyx at least twice as wide as the berry. The flowers are purplish and bell-shaped, and the plant grows upright rather than sprawling.

black walnut

Juglans nigra

EDIBLE nuts

Black walnut trees provide beautiful wood for furniture, but they also produce delicious nuts that have a stronger and fruitier flavor than cultivated walnuts.

How to Identify

The black walnut tree grows up to 100 feet tall. It has elegant, lanceolate, pinnately compound leaves that are 1 to 2 feet long, and the dark brown bark is ropy-looking with deeply furrowed, flattened ridges. The flowers start to appear in spring and produce green, spherical fruits that have a lemon-scent. The fruits have an outer husk with an irregularly furrowed, globular nut inside.

Where and When to Gather

Black walnut trees grow in hardwood forests in moist, well-drained soil. You can often find them around old homesteads. Gather the fruits in October when they fall to the ground.

A black walnut has fallen to the ground with the husk still attached.

The black walnut tree has lance-shaped leaves.

The bark of a black walnut tree is more deeply furrowed than the bark of a hickory or an oak.

How to Gather

If you are gathering the green, unripe fruit for making liqueurs, you will have to use an apple picker or a long stick to knock them down. Gather the ripe fruits by picking them up off the ground after they have fallen from the tree. Storms will often knock them down. When gathering black walnuts, wear gloves or the husk will stain your hands for several weeks. And wear gloves when husking the fruit.

How to Eat

Black walnuts are one of my favorite nuts. They taste like English walnuts but are fruitier and a bit stronger. Getting to the nutmeat is laborious but worth it. First, take off the outer husk. I do this by wearing heavy-duty rubber gloves and, using my hands, I pull the husk off the nut. This is a really messy job, so dress accordingly. The next step is to dry the nuts in their shell for about three weeks in a cool, dry room. They will keep for a very long time once they are dried in their shell. Crack some of the nuts after three weeks to see if they are ready: they should be crisp and not soft or spongy. Then, use the nutmeats right away or store them briefly in the refrigerator—they can go rancid quickly because of the oil in the nuts. Cracking the nuts is probably the most difficult step because the shells are hard to crack. Use a towel and a hammer or a special black walnut cracker. I recommend the nutcracker that Lehman's catalog sells. Black walnuts are great out of hand and in just about any dish, sweet or savory.

How to Preserve

Black walnuts that have been cured (removed from the husk and exposed to air to dry) last for several months in their shell. If you do not take the husk off, the nuts will spoil. Once shelled, black walnuts do not last very long. Refrigerate in an airtight container for up to one week or freeze them in ziplock bags for several months.

Future Harvests

There is no need to limit your harvest of black walnuts.

blueberry

Vaccinium species

EDIBLE fruit

Wild blueberries look just like their cultivated counterparts, but the berries are smaller (the size of pencil erasers) and intensely flavored.

How to Identify

There are two main types of wild blueberry, lowbush (*Vaccinium angustifolium*) and highbush (*V. corymbosum*). Both are hardy perennials in the heath, or heather, family.

Wild lowbush blueberry grows up to 1 foot tall and has short-stalked, alternate leaves that are smooth, elliptical, and 1 to 2 inches long. The five-part white flowers look like little bells. The round berries look just like cultivated blueberries but are smaller. If you look closely at a blueberry, it has a five-part "crown" on the blossom end. Wild blueberry bushes grow in colonies that sometimes form dense thickets. Often times, you will find lowbush blueberries. heavy with fruit, covering ridgetops. They need direct sunlight to form fruits. When they grow in the understory of the forest, they usually do not produce any fruits. Highbush blueberry produces flowers and fruit that look just like those of lowbush blueberry except that the plant grows up to 12 feet tall.

The blooms of wild lowbush blueberry look just like cultivated blueberry flowers.

Where and When to Gather

Blueberries grow in acidic soil in forests, mountains, and open fields. They are commonly found on hills and ridges. The plants usually fruit in mid- to late spring and ripen in June.

How to Gather

Gather blueberries by using your hand and carefully dropping them into a pail or container set on the ground or suspended from your belt. You can also use a plastic bag to harvest them into, but move the berries to a firm-sided container after a while so they do not get crushed. I don't use a blueberry rake, because often blueberries hide underneath the leaves where a rake does not reach.

How to Eat

Wild blueberries are smaller and less juicy than cultivated blueberries, but the flavor is deeper and richer. Blueberries are wonderful fresh, but they also make delicious sauces, jams, and jelly. Besides using them in desserts and pancakes, they can be used to complement rich, fatty meats like duck and pork roast. I also love to pickle blueberries for the sweet-tart flavor.

How to Preserve

If you can find enough berries, make pies, jam, jelly, or syrup. Blueberries store really well in the freezer. Pickling them or drying them slightly to make vinegar is a great way to preserve the harvest.

Future Harvests

You can pick all the blueberries you want. It is almost impossible to pick them all. Leave some for the critters, though.

burdock
Arctium minus

EDIBLE roots, flower stalk

You may be familiar with burdock for two reasons: one, because it is a delicious, mild, nutty-flavored vegetable that is commonly used in Japanese cooking, and two, because the seed burrs stick all over you like Velcro.

How to Identify

Burdock is a large biennial plant that grows in a rosette shape. It has two to five large, rough, ruffled, wedge-shaped leaves that are dark green above and a woolly white underneath. The leaves grow 28 inches long and 14 inches wide on hollow stalks. The green, grooved, flowering stalk grows about 6 feet tall above the basal rosette, with purple composite flowers that look like shaving brushes. The flowers produce round, bristly, clinging burrs that have seeds inside them. Another species, great burdock (*Arctium lappa*), is not that common. Its leaves are rounder and the leaf stem is not hollow.

The large leaves of burdock grow in a rosette.

Where and When to Gather

Burdock loves roadsides, vacant lots, fields, and basically any place where the soil has been disturbed. Collect burdock root only from rosettes that do not have stalks. Usually the best time to dig up the roots is late summer through the fall into spring. The first-year roots are the best; in the second year, they can be used, but they will be a little tougher. The stalks start to appear in late spring and early summer. They can be collected at any time up until the plant starts to flower. When burdock starts to flower, the stalks are too bitter to eat.

How to Gather

Burdock has a thick root that grows very deep into the ground and is difficult to dig up, a lot like sassafras roots. The best way to dig up burdock root is with a shovel. In Japan, they cultivate them so that they are smaller and easier to dig up. I recommend digging burdock root after rain has loosened the soil and in soil that is not rocky. The stalks should be cut from the base of the plant with scissors when 1 to 3 feet high and before the flower appears.

How to Eat

Burdock root has an earthy, nutty, sweet flavor. Traditionally, in Japan, it is an all-purpose vegetable that is used in soups, stews, and stir-fries, and is pickled. The texture of burdock is unique: it is crisp, crunchy, and meaty, which offers a perfect counterpoint to other textures and flavors in dishes. To prepare the root, first scrub off the dirt and then use a vegetable peeler to remove the skin. The root has many excellent medicinal and nutritional properties, including the fact that it is a general detoxifier and immune system stimulant.

The stalks of the burdock plant are perhaps one of the most underrated and underutilized edible parts of a plant. Burdock stalk should first be peeled with a vegetable peeler because the skin is too bitter to eat. Once peeled, the stalk can be eaten raw or cooked. I prefer it cooked because the cooked version has a mild, slightly sweet flavor that is hard to find anywhere else. Use the peeled stalks in soup or stir-fries.

How to Preserve

Store the roots just like you would any other root vegetable. The stalks should be stored in an airtight container in a refrigerator. The roots and stalks can be pickled to prolong the harvest.

Future Harvests

Burdock is one of the most accursed plants because of its seed burrs that stick to anything and everything. Farmers will gladly let you dig the plants out of their pastures. Just make sure that they do not spray them.

butternut

Juglans cinerea
white walnut
`EDIBLE` nuts

This unassuming tree produces delicious nuts that have
a buttery flavor.

How to Identify

Butternut is a medium-size tree that grows
50 to 70 feet tall. It has pinnately compound leaves that are 15 to 30 inches long,
with lance-shaped leaflets growing 2 to
4 inches long. The gray bark has shallow
grooves and broad, wavy ridges. Butternut
flowers when the leaves are developing in
the spring. The female flowers grow at the
tips of branches, while the male flowers
hang in catkins. The fruits that form are
oblong, green, fuzzy, and hang in clusters
of two to five. Inside the green, outer husk
is a nutshell that is deeply furrowed.

Where and When to Gather

Butternut grows in fertile, moist,
well-drained soils in old fields, mixed

Butternuts, hanging from a branch.

The butternut tree has gray, grooved bark.

hardwood forests, and along fencerows. Gather butternuts in late August and into early September.

How to Gather

Gather butternuts from the ground or you can gently shake the tree. You can husk the nuts two different ways. The first is to immediately husk the nuts. Green husked nuts will be difficult to husk. Make sure to wear gloves so that the nuts will not stain your hands. The second way is to let the husk dry on the nut in a well-ventilated, squirrel-proof area, and then the husk becomes brittle, making removal easy. The downside of this method is that the ink from the husk will seep into the nut, altering the flavor. Once the husk is removed, the nut still has to be cracked. You can crack them like a black walnut (see page 68).

How to Eat

My favorite butternuts are the ones that have had the husk removed while still green. The nuts are soft and sweet. Use them in desserts, or just snack on them. The nuts that have the husk dried on them will taste like a black walnut. You can use butternuts like any other nut.

How to Preserve

Butternuts can be stored for a long time in their shell once the husk is removed and the nut is cured. Once the nuts are cracked, they do not last long. Refrigerate for about a week before using them.

Future Harvests

Butternut is increasingly hard to find because of a rapidly spreading disease that kills many of the trees. Consider planting some of the nuts you find, to help restore the tree's numbers.

cat's ear dandelion

Hypochaeris radicata

spotted cat's ear, flatweed, false dandelion

EDIBLE leaves, stem, flowers

Cat's ear dandelion grows so low to the ground that it evades being mowed by a lawnmower—which is a good thing, because the chewy leaves' pleasant bitterness makes you want more.

How to Identify

Cat's ear dandelion grows 10 to 24 inches tall in a rosette with thick, hairy leaves that have wavy, toothed edges. It produces a stalk with yellow, dandelionlike flowers. Cat's ear dandelion blooms after common dandelion. The leaves exude a milky, white sap just like that of common dandelion. Hawkweed is similar, but at the flowering stage, it has leafy stems, while cat's ear dandelion has hairy unbranched stems.

Where and When to Gather

Cat's ear dandelion grows in lawns, fields, pastures, and waste spaces. The best time to harvest the flowers, stems, and young leaves is in early spring.

The rosette of cat's ear dandelion sinks into the ground to avoid harm.

How to Gather

The leaves, stalks, and flowers can all be eaten. The outer leaves tend to be tough. Use scissors to cut the inner leaves.

How to Eat

The chewy inner leaves are the best and have a pleasant bitterness. They are less bitter than dandelion. The stalks with unopened flower buds are delicious blanched or steamed. Use leaves fresh in salads or you can blanch them in boiling water to improve their tenderness. The stems and unopened flower buds can either be blanched or sautéed. The opened flowers, with their bittersweet flavor, make tasty garnishes, or you can batter and fry them.

How to Preserve

The leaves are best used fresh, but the flower buds and stalk can be pickled. Infuse the blooms in simple syrup for their bittersweet flavor. The infused syrup can be used in cocktails or desserts. Store the leaves, stems, and flowers with a damp paper towel on top of them in an airtight container in the refrigerator.

Future Harvests

There is no need to worry about overharvesting.

cattail

Typha latifolia

EDIBLE shoots, male flowers, pollen

Cattail is ubiquitous in moist ditches and in the wetlands of our country. The edible, corndog-shaped male flowers that are densely packed along the top of the flower spike taste similar to corn.

How to Identify

Cattail is a semiaquatic perennial plant that grows 3 to 10 feet tall in dense stands from underground rhizomes. The shoots grow up to 2 feet tall before forming swordlike, pointed leaves that grow tightly around the stalk and are almost 9 feet tall and 1 inch wide. The male and female flowers grow separately on the same flower spike. The pollen-producing male flowers are on top and the female flowers with the seeds are on the bottom.

Where and When to Gather

Cattails grow in sunny, wet, open areas, swamps, ditches, and at the edge of ponds. Gather the shoots in early May and the flowers and pollen in June to July.

The cattail plant has a distinctive oblong seed head.

How to Gather

Gather the shoots by using both hands to pull the plant up. Cut off the tough, upper parts of the shoots and peel off the outermost layer of leaves until you see the soft, white inner core. Cleaning the shoots is very similar to cleaning a leek. The male flower section of the flower spike can simply be clipped off. Treat the corndog-shaped male flowers like you would corn-on-the-cob. You can boil the section as is or cut off the male flowers as you would remove corn from the cob. To gather the pollen, shake the flower heads onto a dropcloth or sheet of paper and pour into a small container.

How to Eat

The shoots taste similar to cucumbers, but with a different texture. Use them any way you would use a cucumber. When you harvest the shoots, they produce a sticky, jellylike substance. This substance can be collected and used to thicken stews. The corndog-looking male flowers can be steamed or simmered. They taste somewhat like corn. The pollen does not taste like much but it is a good source of protein and other nutrients. It is a gorgeous yellow color and can be used like turmeric or annatto for its color, or blended into dough.

How to Preserve

The shoots, pollen, and flowers should be kept in an airtight container in the refrigerator.

Future Harvests

Collecting the flower heads and pollen does not harm the plant, because cattails spread by their rhizomes. Collect only a small amount of shoots and not all of them.

Warning

Cattail shoots look similar to those of several other plants. If you are unsure, look for the old seed heads from last year. Since cattails grow in water, never take any that could be in line with runoff from pollutants, like cattails that grow in a ditch by a road.

chickweed

Stellaria media

hen's inheritance

EDIBLE flowers, leaves, stems

Chickweed tastes like green pea shoots, with a hint of cornlike sweetness. Besides great flavor, the crunchy texture from the stems really stands out.

How to Identify

Chickweed has soft, round stems bearing opposite leaves that are oval to pointy. When growing in abundance, it forms dense mounds. The flowers are tiny, star-shaped, and white, blooming in clusters at the end of the stem. Several types of chickweed grow in the Southeast.

Common chickweed (*Stellaria media*) is the only one with leaves that grow on short stalks. Star chickweed (*S. pubera*) has leaves without stalks. Both species do not have much hair, while mouse-ear chickweed (*Cerastium vulgatum*) is hairy with leaves that do not have stalks. Chickens are, indeed, very fond of chickweed. Star

Chickweed has oval, pointy leaves.

chickweed and mouse-ear chickweed are edible, but the texture is a lot tougher and they are not as palatable as *S. media*.

Where and When to Gather

Chickweed grows where the soil is fertile. You can find it in gardens, lawns, compost piles, and along sidewalks. It starts coming up in November, and by December, it is the perfect size for harvesting. It will grow until late spring, when it starts to bloom. Once it blooms and goes to seed, it becomes stringy and unpleasant to eat.

How to Gather

You can gather chickweed at any time until it goes to seed. Pick either by snipping the whole plant a couple of inches above the ground or by pinching off the tops. This way, the plant will regrow for many harvests.

How to Eat

Chickweed is best eaten raw. Use it in salads or as a garnish. Chickweed is also full of vitamins.

How to Preserve

Chickweed is best eaten fresh. To preserve the freshness, keep it in a refrigerator in an airtight container with a damp paper towel on top. It will last about a week kept this way.

Future Harvests

Even though chickweed likes to get a foothold in areas, it is not invasive. Be sure not to take the whole plant, roots and all. Harvesting by cutting it correctly allows it to grow back.

chicory

Cichorium intybus

`EDIBLE` leaves, root, flowers

Chicory root is often used as a coffee substitute, and the leaves are a delicious salad green.

How to Identify

Chicory is a perennial that grows from a large taproot. The deeply lobed leaves grow 3 to 10 inches long in a basal rosette. The leaf's midrib is often red with many tiny hairs. Chicory is often mistaken for dandelion, which has no hairs on the midrib.

The flower stalk grows up to 4 feet tall with alternate leaves. The flowers are composite and stalkless with a sky blue color. They open for one day at dawn and close by lunchtime. The stunning blue flowers reaching above the meadow grasses signal the presence of the plant.

Chicory has spectacular light blue flowers.

Where and When to Gather

Chicory grows in fields, disturbed soil, and along roads. The leaves are best in early spring and the root is good at any time before flowering.

How to Gather

Clip or pinch off the young leaves and flowers. Use a shovel to dig up the root.

How to Eat

Chicory leaves are best eaten raw. They have a pleasant bitter flavor like dandelion. Citrus and fatty, rich meats cut the bitterness. The flowers can be infused into liquids to impart their bittersweet flavor, and the blue flower petals make a spectacular garnish. The roots can be dried, roasted, and ground to make chicory coffee, like you'll find served in New Orleans. The first-year roots can also be used as a root vegetable.

How to Preserve

The roasted roots can be stored in an airtight container indefinitely. The leaves should be stored in an airtight container with a damp paper towel on top in a refrigerator for up to a week.

Future Harvests

Even though it is a hardy perennial, harvest from a patch where there are others so it will live on in that spot.

chokeberry

Aronia melanocarpa

aronia

EDIBLE fruit

The delicious juice from the fruit of chokeberry tastes like a mix of grape, blackberry, and sour cherry.

How to Identify

Chokeberry is a medium-size deciduous shrub growing 3 to 6 feet tall with grayish brown branches and thin twigs. The elliptical leaves with pointy tips and finely serrated margins are borne alternately on very short leafstalks. The leaves are dark green on top and lighter green underneath, with a shiny appearance. In mid- to late spring, the white flowers appear and look like blackberry blooms. They are very fragrant and produce fruit that hangs in panicles, like a grape cluster, looks like a blueberry, and ripens to a dark, purplish black.

Another chokeberry, *Aronia arbutifolia*, looks very similar to *A. melanocarpa*, but the underside of the leaves has a grayish woolly coating and the ripe berries are red. Both species have edible fruit.

The ripe berries of the chokeberry bush are round and dark purple.

Where and When to Gather

Chokeberry grows in wet, acidic soil in swamps, marshes, bogs, lakeshores, and sometimes dry, sandy soil. You can also find it in urban settings because landscapers often plant the shrubs for their glossy leaves. The berries start to ripen in mid-August and usually last until November. The longer they stay on the bush, the drier they will get, so it is best to pick them as soon as they are ripe.

How to Gather

Handpick the berries into a container.

How to Eat

Chokeberries are highly variable in flavor. Some bushes produce fruit that is small and astringent like a bitter grape flavor. Taste the chokeberries before deciding to pick a bunch of them off a particular plant.

The best way to use the fruit is by making juice, because you remove a lot of the astringency along with the pulp.

To make juice from the berries, boil and mash the fruit in water using a ratio 1:2 (water to berries). Boil for twenty minutes, pour into a fine-mesh strainer lined with cheesecloth, and strain. Once strained, tie the cheesecloth up into a ball and squeeze out as much of the dark purple juice as possible. The juice can be enjoyed as is or sweetened. It can also be frozen into ice cubes, made into jelly, used in a syrup, or made into a sorbet.

How to Preserve

The berries will last for several weeks in your refrigerator.

Future Harvests

There is no need to limit your harvest.

cleavers

Galium aparine

bedstraw

EDIBLE young leaves, stalk, seeds

Have you ever been weeding a flower bed in the spring or summer and come across a green weed that cleaves to your clothes? That is cleavers, which has young hairy leaves and stems with a mild, pealike flavor.

How to Identify

Cleavers is an annual that is found in woodlands, disturbed places, and commonly in shady areas. It grows up to 3 feet tall. Its pale green, narrow leaves grow in whorls of eight with downward-curved bristles, and the stem also has these bristles. The coarse stickiness is not present in the young plants. Starting in June, the plant produces tiny greenish white flowers that grow in loose clusters from the axils of the upper leaves. The fruits start out as green sticky burrs and then turn brown when dry. The whole plant will stick to you and commonly grows in a tangled mess.

The young leaves of cleavers are perfect for a salad.

Where and When to Gather

Cleavers grows in shady areas where the ground has been disturbed. It loves fertile soil like compost piles. Cleavers appears in January and grows until the late summer when it goes to seed. You can gather cleavers at any time up until it blooms.

How to Gather

Harvest young leaves and stalks of cleavers by using scissors to cut just above a whorl of leaves.

How to Eat

Cleavers has a mild, pealike flavor. Before the coarse stickiness appears, the young tops are good raw in a salad. Once the bristles appear, quickly blanch the stalk and leaves to remove the bristles. After blanching cleavers, turn it into a sauce. The seeds can be used as a coffee substitute. Once the seeds turn brown, dry them, then rub the seeds inside a pillowcase to remove the outer coating. Once clean, toast them in a hot pan and grind.

How to Preserve

Fresh cleavers should be kept in an airtight container with a damp paper towel on top in a refrigerator for up to a week. To preserve the harvest, blanch the stalk and leaves, purée into a sauce, and freeze.

Future Harvests

Cleavers is widespread and is considered a weed by some. It can be invasive. Harvest without reserve.

common amaranth

Amaranthus retroflexus

amaranth, redroot pigweed, green amaranth

EDIBLE young leaves, young stem, seeds

Common amaranth is a garden weed that was cultivated by the Native Americans in the Southeast for the nutty seeds and the leaves that taste similar to spinach.

How to Identify

Common amaranth is an annual that grows up to 7 feet tall. The greenish stem is hairy, with leaves that are toothless, coarse, and oval. Tiny green flowers grow in dense clusters. Thousands of seeds are produced. The roots are red, giving the plant one of its common names, redroot.

Several different species of amaranth grow in the wilds of the southeastern United States, with common amaranth being the most often encountered. Spiny amaranth (*Amaranthus spinosus*) is very similar to common amaranth, but with sharp spikes at the nodes on the stem. All amaranths are edible.

These green seed heads of common amaranth are not ready to pick yet.

Where and When to Gather

Common amaranth grows in disturbed soil and especially loves garden soil. As soon as the soil warms, amaranth will spring up. Pick the young leaves and stem in May. Once the flowers start to appear, the stems get too tough to eat. The leaves can still be eaten, but they are not as good as the young ones. The seeds will turn from green to yellow or brown when ripe and ready to gather in September to October.

How to Gather

Gather the leaves and stem by clipping or pinching off. The seeds are harvested by stripping the seed clusters into a container, letting them dry, rubbing them to loosen the seeds from the chaff, and then winnowing the chaff (see Winnowing Seeds and Grain, page 18). The tiny seeds are difficult to winnow from the chaff, but the flavor is excellent.

How to Eat

The leaves and young stem are best cooked. Cook and use the young, nutty-flavored leaves any way you would use spinach. You can also just sauté the whole, young plant. The older leaves can be used like a bay leaf to flavor soups and stews. The seeds have a nutty flavor similar to millet. You can also grind the seeds to make flour or meal.

How to Preserve

Keep the leaves and stem with a damp paper towel on them in an airtight container in the refrigerator. Store dried common amaranth seed in tightly covered jars in a dark, dry place. Stored this way, the seed will keep indefinitely.

Future Harvests

Common amaranth is invasive and self-seeds prolifically, so harvest as much as you want.

Warning

If you are gathering common amaranth from a farmer's field, make sure he does not use artificial fertilizers or chemicals. Common amaranth will pull pollutants from the soil, and these are stored in the plant.

common mallow

Malva neglecta

cheeseweed

`EDIBLE` leaves, flowers, young seed head

Mallow leaves have a sweet flavor throughout the season. They are good raw in salads and excellent as sautéed greens.

How to Identify

Mallow is an annual low-growing plant with leaves that are ¾ inch to 2½ inches across, round or slightly lobed, hairy, with teeth along the margins. They grow alternately along the stems and have long leafstalks. A distinctive feature of the leaves is that they have fanlike pleats. The five-petaled flowers are pink or lavender and grow from the middle of the plant.

The fruits are the identifying characteristic for common mallow. They look like small, flattened wheels of cheese about ⅜ inch in diameter. Each wheel is made up

The distinctive, fan-shaped leaves of common mallow are a wild edible that is often passed by.

of several wedge-shaped segments, and the whole is partially wrapped from the base in a calyx that resembles a five-pointed sheath.

Where and When to Gather

Common mallow grows in disturbed soils and sunny spots near buildings and bushes, at the edges of paths, in lawns and fields, parking lots, and even in pavement cracks. The plant is in season from May through November.

How to Gather

Collect the leaves by pinching or snipping them off near where they attach to the leafstalk. Harvest just the leaves, because the stems are stringy and not appetizing. Collect the flowers the same way as the leaves. They are delicate and best put into a container rather than a bag to protect them until they are served. Harvest mallow fruits when they are still immature and completely green.

How to Eat

Young mallow leaves are good raw in salads. Both young and older mallow leaves are good steamed, sautéed, or briefly boiled. When cooked, the leaves have a mucilaginous texture like okra, which makes them good for thickening soups and stews. You can eat mallow fruits raw or lightly cooked. You can also use them to make a dessert similar to marshmallows. In fact, marshmallows were originally made from the roots of another mallow, *Althaea officinalis*. The pretty flowers are perfect as a garnish on top of salads and other dishes.

How to Preserve

Mallow leaves can be dried and added to gumbo, winter soups, and stews to thicken them. To dry mallow leaves, harvest the top several inches of the plants with the leaves still attached to the branching main stems. Bundle three or four of these stems together and secure them with baling twine or a twist tie. Hang them away from direct light or heat for about a week, after which they should be fully dry. Crumble the leaves into clean, dry jars and cover tightly. The green fruits, which are high in protein, can be pickled and used like capers.

Future Harvests

Common mallow is considered invasive so there is no need to worry about endangering this plant by harvesting it.

cow parsnip
Heracleum maximum
Indian celery
`EDIBLE` leafstalks, flowers, stem, seeds

Cow parsnip has a distinct spicy-sweet aroma and stalks that were traditionally used as a vegetable by Native Americans, so it is sometimes called Indian celery. The peeled stalks have a crunchy texture and a flavor that combines fennel, celery, and clove.

How to Identify

Cow parsnip can grow up to a herculean 9 feet tall, hence the genus name *Heracleum*. The alternate leaves, which are divided into three segments with toothed leaflets, can get to be 1½ feet long. They are rough and hairy, and the hollow leafstalks are winged at the base where they attach to the stems. The stout, densely hairy, hollow stems are grooved. The sweet-smelling flowers are cream colored and grow in flat-topped umbels with five petals. The petals are different sizes, giving each flower a lopsided look. Before the flowers open,

Cow parsnip grows in wet areas.

the buds appear sheathed and swollen, and can be as big as a tennis ball. Each cow parsnip seed is in a winged disc. The seeds are intensely fragrant. The fleshy, off-white roots are also aromatic.

Where and When to Gather

Cow parsnip grows in partial sunlight in moist soils. Look for it along stream banks, and in damp woodlands, marshes, and ditches. The stems and leafstalks are ready to harvest April to May. Collect the seeds green or after they ripen, any time July to October.

How to Gather

Cut off the young stems and leafstalks with shears before the plants flower, and then the sheathed flower clusters. Collect the young leaves when they have just unfurled. Break or cut off whole seed heads and store them in cloth or paper bags until fully dry in an area that is rodent proof.

How to Eat

Every part of cow parsnip is edible and assertively flavored. Although there is some difference in how the various parts taste, they all have a similar savory flavor. They taste similar to celery, but in their own unique way. Treat the edible parts of cow parsnip as a spice. To use the leaf-stalks and flower stalks, first peel them with a vegetable peeler or paring knife. Once peeled, these two ingredients can be used in either a sweet or a savory dish. Some people eat them raw, but I prefer them cooked, either in small amounts added to soups, or candied by boiling them in syrup. Before the flower clusters open, you can chop the whole flower cluster and use it as a cooked vegetable. You can also pickle the peeled stems.

How to Preserve

Young cow parsnip leaves once dried have a lovagelike flavor. The leaf and flower stalks can be candied or pickled. They will keep for months once candied. Store the chopped, dried flower balls and the dry seeds in airtight containers.

Future Harvests

Cow parsnip is a perennial plant, so leave some behind so that it regenerates.

Warning

Poison hemlock (*Conium maculatum*) and water hemlock (*Cicuta maculata*), two lethally dangerous plants in the same family as cow parsnip, have several hairless stems, whereas cow parsnip has a single hairy stem. Be careful handling cow parsnip, because the juice can cause a bad rash if the skin is exposed to sunlight before you can wash it off.

crabapple

Malus angustifolia
southern crabapple

EDIBLE flowers, fruit

Crabapple has a reputation for its tart astringency. I make delicious jelly, wine, and infusions from this underutilized, ancient fruit.

How to Identify

Crabapple is a shrub or small tree growing up to 30 feet tall with thorny branches and leaves 2½ inches long and 1½ inches wide. The fragrant, pastel, five-petaled flowers attract bees and produce yellow-green fruits.

Where and When to gather

Crabapple tends to grow by itself or in thickets along streams, slopes, fencerows, and in old fields. It blooms in mid- to late spring. The fruit ripens in the fall. Both the flowers and fruit can be eaten.

The crabapple tree has fragrant, white and pink blooms.

How to Gather

The green wood can be used for smoking meat or fish. Gather the flowers or wood by cutting. The fruit can be picked from the tree or gathered from the ground once they have fallen.

How to Eat

The flowers, with their strong, floral, slightly applelike aroma, work well when infused in liquids—a good way to capture the fragrance. The fruits are commonly cooked to make jelly or used to make cider. The sourness of crabapple is a good way to balance the sweetness of other fruit.

How to Preserve

The flowers should be stored with a damp paper towel on them in an airtight container in the refrigerator. Store the apples in a cool root cellar or refrigerator. Jelly and cider made from crabapples will store well.

Future Harvests

If you use the flowers, take only some of them, so others are left behind to produce fruits.

crinkleroot

Dentaria diphylla
broadleaf toothwort

EDIBLE leaves, flowers, stem, roots

This plant of the open woods has roots with a wonderful peppery flavor that chefs like to use.

How to Identify

Crinkleroot is a perennial with stems 8 to 16 inches long that grow from a long rhizome. Its three leaves are mostly evergreen, toothed, and prominently veined. The off-white, four-petaled flowers are borne in terminal clusters and turn pink with age.

Where and When to Gather

Crinkleroot grows in fertile soil on wooded slopes and in ravines. Gather the roots at any time of the year. The leaves are best before the plant flowers. The flowers and stem should be gathered between April and May.

Crinkleroot has prominently veined, broad evergreen leaves.

How to Gather

The leaves, flowers, and stem should be gathered by cutting with shears. Do not gather all the leaves or flowers on a plant, but just a little. Gather the roots by digging them up with a shovel. Knock the dirt off and rinse before using.

How to Eat

Crinkleroot's peppery flavor is similar to horseradish. The leaves, stem, and flowers have the same flavor as the roots, but milder. Use them on burgers or sandwiches. The flowers make a pretty garnish and can help tie together a dish with their mild horseradish flavor. Use the root to season soups and stews, and in sauces.

How to Preserve

Store the roots in a refrigerator or a root cellar. Make sure the roots do not dry out. Crinkleroot can also be pickled. The roots can be pulverized and used to make a horseradishlike sauce. Horseradish sauce can be preserved for future use by canning.

Future Harvests

Harvest only from abundant colonies of crinkleroot.

curly dock

Rumex crispus

EDIBLE leaves, stalks, seeds

Curly dock is a ubiquitous weed with tart, sour leaves, crunchy celerylike stalks, and nutty seeds.

How to Identify

Curly dock is a perennial that grows in a rosette of long, narrow leaves 6 to 10 inches long and up to 3 inches wide. The plant has a long, yellowish orange taproot. The leaves have wavy edges and grow on leafstalks 6 inches long. A sheath called an ocrea at the base of the leaves clasps the stems. Curly dock's brownish green flowers are borne in branched clusters atop a stalk that grows up to 5 feet tall. The blossoms become a rusty brown, three-part husk with something called tubercles that look like they should be the seeds but actually are not. The rusty brown color of the seed heads is noticeable from a distance from midsummer well into winter.

In our region, there is another dock called broad-leaved dock (*Rumex obtusifolius*). It looks similar to curly dock but has

The leaves of curly dock have curly edges.

wider leaves that do not curl at the margins. It is also edible, but the flavor is not as good as curly dock.

Where and When to Gather

Curly dock grows in fields, gardens, waste places, and disturbed soil. Gather the leaves in late winter to early spring while the edges are still rolled up. After that, the flavor becomes bitter. The stalks can be gathered at any time up until the plant starts to flower. The seeds can be gathered once the seed heads have dried on the plants and turned a rusty-red color.

How to Gather

Snap off the young leaves by hand. Cut the young flower stalks off near the base. Break or cut off the rust-colored seed heads and put them in a cloth or paper bag.

How to Eat

Curly dock leaves are best cooked. They have a pleasant sour flavor that is similar to that of sorrel. Steam them like you would spinach, or boil them in a big pot of water. The lemony, sour flavor remains after boiling. Use the leaves in quiche, sautéed, or in a stir-fry. If you use them in a stir-fry, add them at the end so the leaves retain their pleasant chewiness. Peel the stalks before using. They have a mild sourness that complements the crunchy, celerylike texture. The seeds can be used, chaff and all, in baked goods or hot cereals.

How to Preserve

The peeled stalks can be pickled, and the leaves can be used to make sauerkraut. The seeds can be stored for up to a year in an airtight container.

Future Harvests

There is no need to limit your harvest.

dandelion

Taraxacum officinale

common dandelion

EDIBLE leaves, flowers, flower buds, root crown, root

Dandelion is not just for kicking their seed heads into the wind. It has several edible parts that have a pleasant bitterness.

How to Identify

Dandelion is a perennial that grows in a rosette with long to short lance-shaped, deeply lobed leaves. The yellow ray-shaped flowers grow atop one hollow, smooth stalk. The flowers go to seed quickly, forming a ball of fluffy seeds. Each seed is like a parachute so it can be blown by the wind far and wide. The taproot is beige with a white core and is long and impossible to dig up whole—part of it always breaks off.

There are no poisonous look-alikes. Some people confuse dandelion with wild lettuce. Dandelion has no hairs on the midrib, a distinguishing characteristic, whereas wild lettuce has hairs on the underside of the midrib.

Dandelion has characteristic deeply lobed, lance-shaped leaves without any hairs on the midrib.

Where and When to Gather

Dandelion grows just about anywhere the soil has been disturbed. It reliably appears from fall to summer.

How to Gather

Gather the leaves before the plant starts to flower. Harvest the flowers, flower buds, and root crown by cutting them off. The taproot needs to be dug.

How to Eat

The young leaves can be eaten raw in salads or cooked. The opened flowers are appealing garnishes, can be made into wine, and you can batter them and fry them. The unopened flower buds can be pickled like capers. The roots are most commonly roasted in the oven and then ground to make a coffee substitute. After roasting, they can also be used as a base flavor in soups, salads, or desserts.

How to Preserve

Use the flowers to make dandelion wine, beer, or vinegar. Pickle the flower buds like capers. Roast the roots to make a coffee substitute.

Future Harvests

There is no need to limit your harvest. Even when digging up the whole plant, some of the root is left behind, but it will take a while to get going again.

daylily

Hemerocallis fulva

orange daylily

`EDIBLE` young shoots, flowers, flower pods, corms

Daylily is a common early summer flowering plant with several edible parts that have surprising flavors.

How to Identify

Daylily is native to Asia and was brought to our country to plant in gardens and flower beds for its showy orange flowers. This plant has escaped cultivation into the wild. The shoots first appear in early spring from underground connected rhizomes called corms. The lime-green shoots grow into a fan shape, and the leaves have linear, parallel veins and taper to a point. The orange, short-stemmed flowers rise above the leaves from a 3-foot-tall leafless flower stalk. The plants spread underground through their corms, forming dense clusters. Each flower lasts only one day, giving the plant its common name.

The shoots of daylily resemble those of poisonous lilies, irises, and daffodils, so

The shoots of the daylily plant are ready for harvesting in the early spring.

Daylily is often grown in gardens for its edible, orange flowers.

beware. Only pick in an area where you have seen the flowers growing year after year and have correctly identified the plant. The orange flowers of daylily are distinctive and do not look like those of other, poisonous lilies.

Where and When to Gather

Daylily comes up in old fields, gardens, roadsides, and the banks of streams. They start to appear in early spring and last for a few weeks into the summer.

How to Gather

Gather the shoots when they are 10 to 12 inches high. They will get tougher when they get bigger. The unopened flower buds can be gathered at any time. The shoots, flower buds, and flowers should be gathered by cutting with shears.

How to Eat

The shoots are tasty grilled, sautéed, boiled, pickled, and poached. Use them like you would a leek. The flower buds taste like green beans. Sauté, pickle, or steam them. The flowers can be used just like squash blossoms. There are many ways to stuff them. Remember to take out the slender stamens inside the flower. Then stuff the blossoms with burrata cheese or crab and panfry them. They are great in soups; just add toward the end of the cooking time. The flowers dry really well and are a traditional ingredient in Chinese cooking. Use the dried flowers in hot-and-sour soup. The corms can be cooked like potatoes, and taste sweet and nutty.

How to Preserve

Pickle the shoots and flower buds and dry the flowers. The corms can be cooked in a fat such as duck fat or extra-virgin olive oil to create a confit. Once prepared this way, the tubers will last for several months stored in the fat they were cooked in.

Future Harvests

Harvest daylily in moderation. If you come across a big patch, thin some out to help the others thrive.

elderberry

Sambucus canadensis

EDIBLE flowers, fruit

Elderberries have a certain mystique, but they are not just for fairy tales. They are also delicious and medicinal, with a light floral fragrance.

How to Identify

Elderberry is a deciduous shrub that grows up to 13 feet high. It has smooth, gray bark and opposite, compound leaves that are 2 to 4 inches long, elliptical, serrated along the margins, and pointed. The white, lacy flowers grow in flat-topped clusters. The fruits start out purple and ripen to black.

Where and When to Gather

Elderberry grows in moist woods, fields, and roadsides. Its blooms start in late June and last for a couple of weeks. Once the flowers give way to the berries, you will want to watch them for a couple of weeks. The berries take several weeks to ripen and are a dark purple, almost black when ripe.

These elderberries are almost ripe.

The blooms of elderberry have a clean, fresh fragrance.

How to Gather

The best way to gather the flowers and berries is to clip or pluck them off at the base of a cluster.

How to Eat

The flowers can be eaten raw, but the best way to capture their fragrance is to infuse them into liquids, such as vinegars and liqueurs. The fragrance is light, floral, and irresistible. The unripe berries can be brined and cured like capers to make them edible. The ripe berries can be used to make all baked goods like pies. Elderberries should be cooked, because they disagree with people when eaten raw. A syrup made from elderberries is an herbal remedy to get rid of colds and flu.

How to Preserve

The flowers should be kept with a damp paper towel on them in an airtight container in the refrigerator. They should be used as soon as possible. Refrigerate the berries as well.

Future Harvests

Only take some of the flowers from an individual elderberry bush, so the bush can produce fruits and continue its life cycle uninterrupted.

evening primrose

Oenothera biennis

EDIBLE first-year taproot, leaves from the stem, young stalks, flower buds, flowers, seeds

Different parts of evening primrose have different flavors. Raw, the root has a wonderful peppery, radishlike flavor. Once cooked, it tastes more like a turnip. The flowers are surprisingly sweet.

How to Identify

Evening primrose gets its name from its flowers which open at night and close by midmorning. It is a biennial that grows in a basal rosette. Its lance-shaped leaves have a pale green midrib tinged with red. The fleshy, white taproot grows over a foot long. In its second year, it produces a flower stalk growing up to 7 feet tall. The alternate leaves on the stalk are lance shaped and are 3 to 6 inches long.

The yellow flower at the top of the stalk is about 1 inch wide and has four petals growing in a circle. Only a few blooms open at a time, and the subsequent seedpods are tiny, hard, reddish brown, and elongated.

Where and When to Gather

Evening primrose grows in sunny, dry, open places, old fields, gardens, at the edges of fields, and in disturbed soil. The taproot can be gathered at any time until

The flowers, leaves, root, and seeds of evening primrose are edible.

the plant starts to flower, and then it gets too tough. Gather the young stalk early in the second year of growth. Start to gather the flower buds and flowers in June. They usually bloom until October. The seeds can be gathered in late October.

How to Gather

Gather the first-year taproot by using a shovel or digging stick. The flowers, flower buds, and seedpods can be picked right off the plant.

How to Eat

Evening primrose roots can be cooked or eaten raw. Most people prefer it cooked. The raw flavor is extremely peppery and spicy, similar to the strongest radish you have ever had. Cooking it lessens the spice.

If you use it in soup, it will thicken the soup like okra does. The root makes great pickles, too. The flower buds are excellent added to cooked vegetables. The flowers, my favorite part to eat, are beautiful and sweet. Use them raw in salads and as a garnish. The seeds are a very tasty and a healthful snack because they contain gamma-linolenic acid.

How to Preserve

Keep all parts of evening primrose in an airtight container in the refrigerator.

Future Harvests

The plant dies after its second year, but you do not want to take all the flowers, flower buds, or seedpods. Leave some behind so it will self-seed.

false Solomon's seal

Maianthemum racemosum

EDIBLE fruit, shoots

False Solomon's seal is a graceful woodland plant that has several edible parts. The shoots are asparaguslike but with a slightly bitter aftertaste. The fruits have a molasses or raisinlike sweet flavor, with a slightly bitter aftertaste.

How to Identify

When they have just popped up in the spring, false Solomon's seal and Solomon's seal, a similar-looking plant, are hard to tell apart. They both start out with tightly rolled-up leaves atop long, round stems. At first, the leaf roll points upward. Shortly after, the still-furled leaves bend at an angle. As the plant matures, the single stem grows into an arc from one to several feet long. The leaves grow alternately along the stem and have smooth margins. The leaf veins are parallel.

Unlike Solomon's seal flowers, which hang down in pairs from along the stalk, false Solomon's seal cream-colored flowers

The fruit of false Solomon's seal hangs at the tip of the stalk.

are clustered at the tips of the stems. Fruits are small (less than ¼ inch) and round, starting off a gold-bronze color and turning red as they ripen. Each fruit has a single seed. The fruit of false Solomon's seal is edible, but the fruit of Solomon's seal is not. Underground, the off-white to slightly beige rhizomes grow horizontally and are marked with numerous rings. On the upper surface of the rhizomes, round dents mark where last year's plants emerged from the roots.

Where and When to Gather

False Solomon's seal is usually a woodland species that likes to grow at the edge of forests and on the sides of roads where trees and bushes grow. It is also sometimes planted as an ornamental in gardens with partial shade. Collect the shoots in spring before the leaves unfurl. Harvest the fruit once it has turned red.

How to Gather

Harvest the shoots when the leaves are still tightly furled. They are best when upright, but you can harvest them when they've started to bend sideways. Start at the base and gently work your way up, bending the stalk and feeling for the point at which it breaks with ease. With younger plants, this point will be near the soil level. On older plants, it will be farther up the stalk. The berries can be picked off the plant by hand. Berries from some plants are better than others, so try several plants from different areas.

How to Eat

Remove the leaves from false Solomon's seal shoots, because they are not good to eat. Cook the shoots by sautéing or blanching them quickly like you would asparagus. The fruit is usually eaten as a snack.

How to Preserve

The cleaned shoots should be stored in an airtight container in a refrigerator for up to a week. You can make vinegar with the fruit.

Future Harvests

Do not overharvest false Solomon's seal. Only collect where you find a healthy patch of it. If there are just a few plants, leave them alone. When you do find a thriving patch, collect no more than 20 percent of it.

Warning

You might read elsewhere that the ripe berries are a laxative. I have never encountered that problem as long as I spit out the seed.

field garlic

Allium vineale

field onion, onion grass, wild garlic

EDIBLE leaves, bulbs

Field garlic covers fields and open areas in the fall, winter, and spring with its strong onion-flavored leaves that look like chives. Why go to the store for chives when they grow all around you?

How to identify

Field garlic has long, slender, tubular, green leaves that grow up to 2 feet tall from underground bulbs. The bulbs look like tiny onions that grow together. They propagate by splitting off from each other and forming a clump. Field garlic blooms in late spring with pink to white flowers in pom-pom clusters. The flowers are replaced by bulbets (or bulbils, small bulbs that grow on a stem) that will grow thread-like green tendrils. The bulbets will eventually fall to the ground and grow into new plants.

Wild onion (*Allium canadense*) is similar, but it has flat leaves and grows only to

A clump of field garlic reveals its round, hollow leaves.

14 inches. It grows in fields, parks, waste places, and moist woods. The nodding wild onion (*Allium cernuum*) has a bend in the flower's stalk tip and no bulbets.

Where and When to Gather

Field garlic grows in fields, disturbed soil, and open woods. It starts coming up in the fall and can be harvested during the winter and spring. Be extremely careful about harvesting alliums from vacant lots in the city, because if there are heavy metals in the soil, they will have absorbed those pollutants.

How to Gather

You can gather field garlic anytime it is growing. The whole plant from the roots to the top can be eaten. Harvest by digging up the whole plant or snipping the green tops off.

How to Eat

Field garlic tastes like pungent onions with a hint of garlic. Use the green tops like chives. The bulbs with roots attached are excellent fried in a tempura batter. Chop up the whole plant to use in broths and soups. Use field garlic in any way you would use onions or garlic.

How to Preserve

Pickle the bulbs with a basic pickling brine or use in kimchi. You can also dry the whole plant and grind it into an oniony garlic powder. Broth made with field garlic can be frozen.

Future Harvests

Field garlic is a prolific self-seeder. Even so, do not dig all of them up in one location. If you just clip the green tops off, they will regrow, ensuring a long harvest.

Warning

Nothing that smells like garlic or onion is poisonous. However, some other members of the lily family are poisonous. The most dangerous look-alike is fly poison (*Amianthium muscaetoxicum*), which has an onionlike bulb that grows into a smooth stem topped with white to green, six-petaled flowers that appear in vertical clusters along the stem. This plant is extremely toxic. Do not even touch it! Other poisonous lilies include death camas (*Zigadenus* species). You will want to study these plants to fully know their differences, for field identification.

field mustard

Brassica rapa

wild turnip

EDIBLE flowers, seeds, seedpods, leaves, roots

In the early spring, field mustard fills fields, pastures, and gardens with its yellow flowers that have a spicy mustard-green flavor. My favorite parts are the flowers and flower buds, which are sharp and spicy. Field mustard greens taste similar to cultivated mustard greens.

How to Identify

Field mustard grows in a basal rosette with a stem that reaches up to 3 feet tall. Smooth, green pointy leaves clasp the stem and grow up to 20 inches long. The leaves at the base are deeply lobed, and farther up the stem they are teardrop-shaped. Mustard flowers have four yellow petals in

When in full bloom, field mustard is tall with small yellow flowers up the stem.

the distinctive cross pattern that identifies plants in the mustard family, Brassicaceae (see *Brassica*, page 63). The flowers grow in clusters, and before they open, the green flower buds look like broccoli florets. Mustard's slender seedpods have a narrow, pointed tip.

Where and When to Gather

Field mustard starts appearing in September and grows until late May in fields and open meadows. The greens are best before the plant starts to flower, when they will develop an unpleasant bitterness. Once established, the plant self-seeds prolifically.

How to Gather

You can gather field mustard at any time. All parts of the plant can be eaten. Harvest them by cutting with scissors, or digging the roots up.

How to Eat

The flowers are good raw as part of a salad or as a garnish for a dish. The buds are excellent pickled, sautéed, or stir-fried. The greens are best before the plant starts to flower, when they develop an unpleasant bitterness. I love to use the greens in a stir-fry.

How to Preserve

Keep any part of field mustard with a damp paper towel on top in an airtight container in the refrigerator. You can use the seeds to make your own mustard. Pickle the flower buds and root, and use the leaves in kimchi.

Future Harvests

There is no need to limit your harvest of this invasive plant.

field thistle

Cirsium discolor

`EDIBLE` young leaves, stalk, root

Do farmers a favor (with permission) and harvest the field thistles that grow all over their pasture. They will thank you gladly.

How to Identify

Field thistle is a biennial 3 to 7 feet tall with leaves that are 4 to 8 inches long. The leaves are deeply lobed with big spines and are white-woolly on the underside. The 2-inch flower heads are pinkish purple. Another thistle in our region, bull thistle (*Cirsium vulgare*), is similar but the leaves are wider.

Where and When to Gather

Field thistle grows in pastures, fields, and disturbed soil. It starts appearing in the wintertime and grows until the fall. Field thistle spends one or more years as a basal rosette, storing energy, before sending up a flower stalk and dying. The midribs of the leaves are at their best in the spring and fall. The stalk can be gathered in the spring

Every two years, field thistle starts as a basal rosette.

and summer at any time up until the plant produces a flower. The root should be gathered in the fall and should not have a stalk.

How to Gather

Gather the leaves by wearing gloves and stripping the leaf down to the midrib. Break off the stalk at the base of the plant. Gather the root by digging up the plant.

How to Eat

Use the crisp midribs like celery. The peeled stalks can be eaten raw or cooked. The flavor is mild and slightly sweet. Field thistle root can be eaten raw or cooked. It tastes like burdock, but better.

How to Preserve

To preserve freshness, store field thistle with a damp paper towel in an airtight container in the refrigerator. The midribs, stalk, and root can be pickled. The root can also be shaved very thin and dried.

Future Harvests

Field thistle is fairly hard to get rid of. Many farmers have it all over their pastures. Animals do not graze thistles, but the plant is valuable to many creatures. Numerous species of butterflies, bees, and birds (like American goldfinch) are attracted to the showy lavender-pink flowers for their nectar and seeds, and for thistle down for nesting material.

garlic mustard

Alliaria petiolata

hedge garlic

`EDIBLE` young shoots, young leaves, flower buds

The young leaves, young shoots, and flower buds of garlic mustard have a strong garlicky mustard flavor that can be used for soups, stews, and meat dishes.

How to Identify

Garlic mustard is a biennial that grows in a basal rosette up to 3 feet tall. It has kidney- or heart-shaped leaves that grow up to 2½ inches wide and are coarsely toothed. The flowering stalk shoots up in the second year of the plant's growth. The flowers at the top of the round, smooth stalk look similar to other mustard flowers: they are small, white, and four-petaled and produce four-part pods containing numerous dark, elongated seeds.

Crush the leaves with your hand to release the strong, garlicky mustard fragrance.

Where and When to Gather

Garlic mustard grows in rich soil in the understory of forests. The best time to gather is March through May.

How to Gather

Gather garlic mustard by pulling the whole plant out of the ground. By doing this, you are helping the forest by removing an extremely invasive plant.

How to Eat

The young leaves can be turned into pesto or used sparingly as a base in soups or stews. The young shoots are milder than the leaves. Pull off any leaves from the shoots and lightly boil or steam the stems. The flower buds can be used as a topping for roast beef sandwiches and hot dogs. The leaves of the first-year rosettes and mature plants are usually too bitter to use.

How to Preserve

Keep garlic mustard with a damp paper towel on top in an airtight container in the refrigerator.

Future Harvests

Garlic mustard is an extremely invasive weed that chokes out native vegetation. Take as much as you want.

ginkgo

Ginkgo biloba
maidenhair tree

`EDIBLE` nuts

The ginkgo tree is famous for its fruit which, although horrible-smelling, contains a nutritious edible nut with a complex nutty flavor. It can be sweet or slightly bitter with a subtle stinky cheese flavor. Once you eat one, it is hard to stop!

How to Identify

Ginkgo is a tall, slender tree growing up to 90 feet with a gray, furrowed bark. The interesting fan-shaped leaves are broad and lobed. There are male and female trees, which are very hard to tell apart when they are young, so you may not know which you have in front of you. Most landscapers want to plant only the male tree because of the fruit that the female tree produces.

The ginkgo tree has leaves with a distinctive fan shape.

The fruit smells like something rotten. Its jellylike husk is soft, orange, and extremely smelly. Inside is a nutshell containing a small, oval nut.

Ginkgo, a tree from China, was once thought to be extinct. Then, in the late 1700s, explorers discovered a few trees in a monastery. The tree soon became popular because of its beauty and healthful nuts. It is widely believed that an extract of the leaves stimulates the immune system and improves memory, and that the nuts enhance your circulation. You can find different kinds of ginkgo products at health food stores.

A large older ginkgo tree has craggy bark.

Where and When to Gather

Ginkgo is a graceful ornamental tree that is planted in parks, yards, and along streets. Gather the fruit in the autumn when they fall to the ground. You will often find them under the tree after a storm.

How to Gather

Only gather ginkgo fruit wearing gloves. Otherwise, you will have a very hard time getting the smell off your hands. In fact, your vehicle will smell as well. I recommend transporting the fruit for only a short time with all the windows down. Clean the outer fruit off the nuts. Do this work outside. Then bake the nuts in their shell in a low oven (200°F) for thirty to sixty minutes until the white shells are dry. The shells are thin and will crack open like a pistachio. The soft nuts become rich after roasting.

How to Eat

Ginkgo nuts should only be eaten cooked. In Asia, people use them in just about anything. They are a classic component with noodles and vegetables in a broth. The nuts are not crunchy like other nuts, but are more like a savory vegetable. Once baked, the nuts should be used immediately or frozen.

How to Preserve

Store baked ginkgo nuts in an airtight container in the refrigerator for no more than a week. If you do not plan on using all of them, freeze them.

Future Harvests

There is no need to limit your harvest.

Warning

Be cautious when eating ginkgo nuts for the first time. Eat only a small amount. Some people get headaches and experience trouble breathing from consuming ginkgo.

glasswort
Salicornia europaea
marsh samphire, sea bean
`EDIBLE` stems

While walking along the ocean beach, you may notice there is a lot of vegetation growing at the edge of the shore, especially in salt flats and marshes. You will probably find glasswort there, which is crunchy and salty.

The crunchy stems of glasswort are edible.

How to Identify

Glasswort is a low-growing plant with erect, fleshy stems that branch out, growing 4 to 20 inches tall. If you look closely, you can see that the stems are segmented and have tiny lobes instead of leaves. Tiny green flowers appear in the upper joints of the stems in July. Glasswort turns a pinkish red in the fall.

Where and When to Gather

Glasswort grows in salt flats that are flooded from time to time. The best time to gather the stems is in March to June when the plants are young and tender. Later, the core gets woody, but you can still chew on the softer part of the stem.

How to Gather

To gather glasswort, use scissors to cut the stems.

How to Eat

I like glasswort stems raw. You can also boil them very briefly to temper the salinity. Glasswort works well with pasta, seafood, and simply sautéed with butter.

How to Preserve

Keep glasswort in an airtight container in the refrigerator. Glasswort pickles really well.

Future Harvests

Cut glasswort stems so that it regrows for a continuous harvest, and do not pull up the whole plant.

goldenrod
Solidago species

EDIBLE leaves, flowers

The yellow flowers of goldenrod bloom at the same time as ragweed during hay fever season. But goldenrod does not cause hay fever like ragweed does. The leaves and flowers make an excellent, mild but tasty tea.

How to Identify

There are several goldenrod species in the genus *Solidago*. They have similar flowers and leaves, but with different shapes. Goldenrod's unbranching central stems grow 2 to 6 feet tall and, like the leaves, are hairy. The alternate leaves are lance-shaped, 2 to 6 inches long, and may or may not have serrated margins. The tiny mustard-yellow flowers grow in a loose cluster called a panicle at the tip of the tall stems. Goldenrod spreads by the roots, forming colonies, so you will often see fields of them.

Giant goldenrod has beautiful yellow flowers in late summer.

Where and When to Gather

Goldenrod grows in full to partial sun. Look for it on hillsides, roadsides, in city parks—any open area with disturbed soil. Collect the tops of just-opened flowers plus several inches of the leafy stems when the plants are just beginning to bloom in August to September.

How to Gather

Break or cut off the top foot or so of a goldenrod stalk.

How to Eat

The best way to use goldenrod is by making a tea with it. Pour boiling water over the fresh flowers and fresh or dried leaves, then cover and steep for ten minutes. The tea can also be used to poach seafood, like lobster or scallops, or to make a refreshing sorbet.

How to Preserve

Goldenrod leaves dry well but the flowers do not. Bundle several stems with the leaves attached, and hang in a place with good air circulation until they are completely dry. Then carefully remove the crumbly leaves and store in an airtight container.

Future Harvests

There is no need to limit your harvest.

gooseberry

Ribes species

EDIBLE fruit

Gooseberries are in the same family as currants and grow in the
same way, but the bushes have thorns. Do not let the bristles on the
gooseberry fruit deter you from making something with its sweet
and sour flavor. Gooseberries make dynamite pies and jam.

Gooseberry fruit comes in different colors: red, light green, and black.

How to Identify

Gooseberry is a small bush growing 2 to 5 feet tall with arching branches. The maple-shaped leaves are sharply toothed and grow alternately on thorny stems. Gooseberry flowers are yellow-green and grouped together in dangling, long clusters called racemes. The semitranslucent, globular fruit hangs in the same arrangement. Depending on the species, the fruit may be bright red, light green, or black. Gooseberries are usually covered in small bristles, but some can be smooth.

Where and When to Gather

Gooseberries grow along meadow borders, stream banks, and as garden escapees along property edges that are adjacent to woodlands. They are one of the earliest fruits to ripen, usually in late spring or early summer, around the same time as strawberries.

How to Gather

Pinch off the hanging fruit clusters where they attach to the woody stems.

How to Eat

Gooseberries are high in pectin, the stuff that makes jellies gel, so they can help a jam or other preserve made with low-pectin fruit, such as a strawberry, to set up. They have a sweet-sour flavor that is excellent as a sauce. Cooking the gooseberries softens the bristles. Besides sauces and jellies, gooseberries make wonderful pies and other pastries. They are also used in mixed drinks.

How to Preserve

Gooseberries freeze well, and the frozen fruit works just as well as fresh in jams, jellies, and sauces, which may be canned (see Preserving Food by Canning, page 19).

Future Harvests

There is no need to limit your harvest of gooseberry.

greenbrier

Smilax species

catbrier, stretcherberry

EDIBLE young leaves, young tips, roots

Walk through an overgrown field in spring and you are likely to brush up against greenbrier, which is a thorny vine with very tender edible stem tips that taste like asparagus.

How to Identify

Greenbrier is a perennial vine found in meadows, roadsides, open woodlands, and disturbed soil. It especially loves brushy fields. It is a long vine with green thorns, tendrils, and heart-shaped 4-inch-long leaves. The six-petaled flowers are yellow-green and grow in flat-topped clusters. The plant bears edible berries, but they don't taste very good. The root looks like cultivated ginger, but thicker. The single vine usually grows from a clump of roots.

Greenbrier is a vining edible plant.

Where and When to Gather

Greenbrier appears in early to mid-spring and grows until fall. The best time to gather the leaves and tips is in spring, when they are green and tender. The roots can be gathered at any time.

How to Gather

You can use your hands to break off the vine tips like you would asparagus, or use scissors to cut them off. Gather the young leaves by snipping with scissors. Gather the roots by using a shovel. The lightest colored of the roots are the best ones to dig.

How to Eat

Use the tender, young, green tips as you would asparagus. The flavor is very similar, but stronger. Cook them only briefly, to retain the crunch. The young leaves have a pleasant sweet-sour flavor. Use them raw in salads or cook them by lightly grilling or quickly blanching them. The roots are full of starch, which thicken soups and stews. They were also used by early settlers to make root beer. They would mix the root with molasses and water in a big tub, throw in a few seeds of parched corn or rice, and after a slight fermentation would season it with sassafras.

How to Preserve

The tips of greenbrier are excellent pickled. Once you pick the tips or leaves, place them in an airtight container in a refrigerator. The roots can be sliced in thin pieces and dried for later use. Store the dried roots in an airtight container at room temperature.

Future Harvests

Where greenbrier grows with abandon in fields, there is no need to limit your harvest. But use restraint, and let the plant mature.

hackberry

Celtis laevigata

sugarberry, sugar hackberry

`EDIBLE` fruit

If you are walking along a city street in the Southeast in fall or winter and notice an odd tree that has smooth bark with bumpy ridges all over it, chances are it is a hackberry tree. Look around on the ground for the fruit, which has an edible dark red shell that crunches like candy.

How to Identify

The hackberry tree grows up to 90 feet tall and is a popular shade tree in our region. It has a straight trunk and smooth bark with distinctive, narrow, high, corky ridges. The leaves grow 3 to 6 inches long with shallowly toothed edges, except along the leaf base, where they are smooth. You might notice several wartlike growths on the leaves, which are caused by an insect and are called hackberry nipple galls. Small, white flowers appear in early spring at the same time as the leaves. The fruits start to ripen in September to a dark purple-brown. The fruit is the size of a pea, with a large seed surrounded by a thin layer of sugary pulp and the crunchy shell.

The distinctive bark of the hackberry tree has corklike ridges.

The hackberry tree bears small fruit.

Where and When to Gather

The hackberry tree grows along sidewalks in cities and in river valleys along floodplains. Gather hackberry fruits starting in October. They will keep ripening till January. My favorite time to gather them is in December and January, when they are the sweetest.

How to Gather

Gather hackberries by either knocking the fruit down from the tree or by picking them up off the ground.

How to Eat

Hackberries are very unassuming. Who knew that their outer shell gets crunchy like M&M candy? It really does! The flavor is somewhere between a date and squash. The big seed inside the shell is edible, but it is often too hard to chew. Since there is not much pulp between the shell and the seed, the best thing to do is to mash the shell and seed with a mortar and pestle. The result should be like a stiff cookie dough. You can eat this "candy" as is, or even make a brittle out of it. Or take the hackberry mash and boil in water for thirty minutes, then strain it through cheesecloth to produce a thick orange-brown liquid that has a rich, hearty flavor. The resulting liquid can be used to make a simple syrup and as a base for sauces or soups.

How to Preserve

Since hackberries have very little liquid in them, they last a long time. There is no need to refrigerate the fruit.

Future Harvests

There is no need to limit your harvest of the fruit. It is impossible to collect all of them.

hawthorn

Crataegus species

`EDIBLE` fruit

Hawthorn fruit has a delicate flavor and makes rosy-colored infusions.

How to Identify

Hawthorns are shrubs or small trees that grow 10 to 30 feet tall. Their leaves are simple, 1 to 2 inches long, and usually lobed. Hawthorn leaves are variable in shape, alternate, and have toothed margins. The flowers, which bloom in flat clusters, look something like apple or cherry blossoms. They are white to pale pink with five petals and bloom in mid-spring. Hawthorn fruits look like little apples hanging in sparse clusters, and are usually red but sometimes red-purple. The long, stout, sharp thorns are a

The hawthorn bush produces edible fruit.

characteristic feature of the plant. The number of seeds in hawthorn fruit can vary from one to five.

Where and When to Gather
Hawthorn grows in full sun or partial shade, and loves open hillsides, pastures, and stream banks. It is also widely planted in city parks as a decorative shrub or tree. Gather the fruit when it is fully ripe in early summer.

How to Gather
The easiest way to collect hawthorn fruit in quantity is to wait until the fruit has started falling from the tree. Lay down a dropcloth and gently shake the trunk. You can also pick the ripe fruit directly from reachable branches.

How to Eat
Hawthorn fruit is usually used for infusing its delicate flavor into vodka or another clear, neutral alcoholic beverage and imparting the color of the fruit's skin. You can use the fruit in recipes that call for removing the seeds, but they are laborious to remove so you may want to use a food mill.

How to Preserve
Infuse the fruit into liqueurs.

Future Harvests
There is no need to limit your harvest.

henbit

Lamium amplexicaule

dead nettle

`EDIBLE` leaves, stem, flowers

Henbit is a pretty annual with a pleasant, herbal, nutty flavor. The flavor is at its best during the fall and early winter.

How to Identify

Henbit is a small, downy plant in the mint family that grows up to 16 inches tall. The rounded, bluntly toothed leaves grasp the square stem that branches at the base. The flowers are pinkish purple and tubular.

Henbit is sometimes confused with purple dead nettle or ground ivy. All three are in the mint family, Lamiaceae. They look somewhat similar, but henbit has heart-shaped, jagged leaves and purple dead nettle has triangular leaves. Ground ivy, which is also edible, grows along the ground and never gets as tall as henbit, and ground ivy leaves smell like mint while henbit does not have a fragrance.

Where and When to Gather

Henbit grows in full sun and in shady spots. It thrives in disturbed soils, and I

Pinkish purple flowers project from the tops of the henbit stems.

find more of it growing as a weed in parks, gardens, lawns, and on farms than I do in wilderness areas. It starts to appear in early fall as the days start to cool. It grows all winter in the South until warm spring weather turns it stringy and bitter.

How to Gather

Gather henbit before and after it has flowered in the early spring. Harvest the plant parts by snipping or breaking them off.

How to use

Use the young leaves and tops in salads. Henbit also holds up well in cooking. The stems are crunchy, and the mild leaves have a ruffled, chewy texture. Use the herbal, nutty flavor to balance out creamy, smooth flavors.

How to Preserve

Henbit works well as a base for pesto or as an ingredient in ravioli filling. Both creations are easy to freeze or to can. You could also purée with water or extra virgin olive oil as a sauce and freeze it.

Future Harvests

There is no need to limit your harvest of henbit. The plant self-seeds prolifically. Do not let it go to seed in your garden unless you want a blanket of henbit, which is quite invasive and hard to get rid of. Invasive species of plants are not a good contribution to your compost pile.

hickory

Carya species

EDIBLE nuts, bark

Even though hickory nuts are notorious for being hard to crack and shell, the nutmeat inside is worth it for its distinctive, sweet, nutty flavor.

How to Identify

Three hickory species prevalent in the South produce good nuts. Mockernut hickory (*Carya tomentosa*) is the most common. It grows up to 90 feet tall and has alternate, compound leaves up to 1 foot long, with serrated lance-shaped leaflets growing on reddish brown twigs. The bark is shallowly furrowed, and the furrows form diamond shapes. The tree produces male and female flowers in the spring. The male flowers are in the form of catkins that droop down, and the female flowers grow at the tip of branches. The fruit has an outer husk that will split apart when ripe, revealing an almost round nut 1/2 to 1 1/2 inches long.

Another regional hickory is the shellbark hickory (*Carya laciniosa*), which has the biggest leaves and nuts of all the hickories. Shagbark hickory (*C. ovata*) is very similar to shellbark hickory in that they both have shaggy bark that peels in strips. While the nuts from the shagbark hickory tree are smaller, many people say that they are the best tasting. Pignut hickory (*C. glabra*)

A hickory nut, its shell open, lies beneath a tree.

The vertical, shaggy bark is an identifying feature of shagbark hickory.

A close-up view of this mockernut hickory tree reveals its ropy bark.

produces nuts that look like figs. They are too bitter for human consumption, but apparently animals, including pigs, love them.

Where and When to Gather

Hickory grows in forests, open fields, at the edge of woods, and in any well-drained soil. The nuts start to form in early summer but are hard to see until they are bigger in August. Start looking for hickory nuts in late September. When nuts mature, usually in October, the nut's outer husk will split open. The bark of the shagbark hickory is the best to use. Gather it at any time.

How to Gather

Hickory nuts are knocked to the ground by wind and passing storms. Gather them off the ground. The husk comes off easily, and then the nut needs to cure for at least three weeks. They take about the same time or a little bit longer to cure than black walnuts. When they are ready, you can crack them with a towel and hammer or by using a nutcracker (as for black walnuts, page 68). Gather shagbark hickory bark from fallen trees or from the ground where the tree has shed it.

The mockernut hickory tree has elliptical leaves.

How to Eat

Hickory nuts have a complex flavor. You know it is a hickory nut, but you can't quite describe the flavor. They are slightly sweet with a classic tree nut flavor. You can use them raw or cooked—as you would any other nut. Once the nuts are shelled, they will go bad fairly quickly because of the high oil content. The bark from shagbark hickory trees can be used to make a syrup. Scrub the bark to clean off any dirt or lichens. Put the cleaned bark inside a pot and cover with water. Bring the water to a boil over high heat, and then turn down the heat to medium-low and simmer until the water turns a dark amber color. Use this flavored water to make a simple syrup, which should be smoky, earthy, and complex.

How to Preserve

Store the nuts in their shell for three to six months until ready to use, or refrigerate the cracked nuts in an airtight container in a refrigerator for up to a week. Nuts in the shell can be stored for at least four months and probably longer. They will keep for a few months in the freezer. The syrup can be canned for later use.

Future Harvests

There is no need to limit your harvest of the nuts, but leave some for the animals. Never take bark off of living trees because that opens the door for insect damage to the tree.

hoary bittercress

Cardamine hirsuta
hairy bittercress

`EDIBLE` leaves, stems, flowers

Walking along the sidewalk in the city during the wintertime, you may notice a small plant with a round, puffy shape that piques your curiosity. It's hoary bittercress. The leaves look like tiny watercress leaves, and indeed, they have a pleasing peppery flavor like watercress.

How to Identify

Hoary bittercress is a small, low-growing annual with small, round leaves 1 to 3 inches long growing in a rosette. As the plant grows, it develops an upright or nodding stem that produces tiny, white flowers. When hoary bittercress goes to seed, the capsules explode and catapult seeds everywhere. The word "hoary" refers to the white flowers that are produced.

This hoary bittercress plant looks perfect for harvest.

Where and When to Gather

Hoary bittercress grows any place where the soil is bare or has been disturbed. It is a common weed in gardens, lawns, and sidewalks. The best time to collect it is January through March.

How to Gather

Use scissors to cut the leaves, flowers, and stems. You can cut a good bit of the plant and it will grow back.

How to Eat

Hoary bittercress has a horseradishlike, peppery flavor similar to watercress. It goes well with strongly flavored foods like game meats. It is a tasty companion to citrus in a salad.

How to Preserve

Pickle hoary bittercress using a basic pickling brine or use it in kimchi. You can also purée and freeze it for later use as a sauce.

Future Harvests

Even though hoary bittercress self-seeds well, do not take all of it. If you do, you will start to see less and less of it.

honeysuckle

Lonicera japonica
Japanese honeysuckle

EDIBLE flowers

I love when honeysuckle starts to bloom because it smells like summer. The hot, humid, summer air in the South is filled with its heady sweet fragrance. I love to use the fragrant blooms to make an infusion.

How to Identify

Honeysuckle is a vining perennial that comes up in fields, roadsides, forests, and disturbed areas. It has opposite, oval leaves with straight edges. The flowers start out white and turn yellow. The yellow flowers have more honey in them.

Where and When to Gather

Honeysuckle grows in fields, roadsides, forests, and disturbed areas. It starts to bloom in May and flowers sporadically through the summer, depending on rainfall.

The sweet nectar of honeysuckle blooms can be made into a heavenly syrup.

How to Gather

Gather the yellow blooms, which are the sweetest, anytime they are present. Pick them by plucking the flower from the vine. The blooms once picked do not last more than a day.

How to Eat

You can suck the honey out of the stem end of the honeysuckle flowers for a trailside treat. But you will want to capture the fragrance by infusing the blooms into a liquid. Honeysuckle syrup is delicious and easy to make. Honeysuckle can be infused into butter, milk, vodka, or any kind of liquid.

How to Preserve

Infuse honeysuckle blossoms into syrup, butters, and alcoholic beverages.

Future Harvests

There is no need to limit your harvest. Once established, honeysuckle is hard to get rid of.

Japanese knotweed

Polygonum cuspidatum

EDIBLE young shoots

Japanese knotweed shoots, which emerge in spring, have a delicious flavor similar to rhubarb.

How to Identify

When Japanese knotweed emerges in spring, its hollow shoots spring straight up with a few leaves still tightly furled at the tips. The skin of the shoots, as well as that of the older stalks, is pale green mottled with reddish spots. The shoots, and later the mature branching stems, are jointed with prominent, swollen nodes, where the leaves emerge in older plants. The

Harvest Japanese knotweed stalks when they are young and tender.

This Japanese knotweed plant is too old to harvest.

leaves of Japanese knotweed are shaped like a gardener's trowel and are almost as wide as they are long, pointed on one end and almost flat or gently curved across the other end. The leaves have leafstalks and get 4 to 6 inches long when mature. The plants will eventually branch out and grow 4 to 8 feet tall. The small, dry, triangle-shaped, one-seeded fruits never open to release the seed, which is about ⅛ inch across, tan to brown, and glossy. The roots are large, woody, and convoluted.

Where and When to Gather

Japanese knotweed loves disturbed and rocky soils. It will grow in both partial shade and full sun. It favors urban areas like parks, but you will also find it along-side roads in the country. Collect Japanese knotweed shoots in March when they are thick and unbranched.

How to Gather

Cut the young shoots off a couple of inches above the ground. If the plants are more than a foot high but still unbranched, harvest by trying to snap them off by hand. Just like with asparagus, the point at which they snap off easily with a clean break marks the separation between the tender, edible upper part of the shoot and the tough, woody lower part.

How to Eat

To use the young shoots, cut off the leafy tips and compost or discard that bit as well as any nascent leaves at the nodes. With very young, tender shoots, that may be all the prep you need. Older shoots may need to be peeled if their skin is already getting a little stringy.

Use Japanese knotweed in any recipe that calls for rhubarb. The taste isn't identical, but the sourness and texture are similar. Knotweed has a greener flavor, and so I like to combine it with other sweeter fruits. You can also use Japanese knotweed in savory dishes. It works well puréed in soup. Raw Japanese knotweed adds a pleasantly sour flavor and crunch to salads, especially salads that contain rice. I love to make dolmas using wild grape leaves, stuffed with a mixture of lamb, rice, and Japanese knotweed. You can make Japanese knotweed wine using a rhubarb wine recipe.

How to Preserve

Japanese knotweed can be frozen without blanching. Make sure to peel and chop it before freezing. It can also be pickled and made into a sorbet.

Future Harvests

There is no need to limit your harvest of this extremely invasive plant.

Jerusalem artichoke

Helianthus tuberosus
sunchoke
EDIBLE tubers

You may be familiar with this relative of the sunflower from cookbook recipes. Jerusalem artichoke is cultivated, but it also grows wild. The tuber is edible and slightly sweet, like a cross between a radish and an artichoke.

How to Identify

Jerusalem artichoke is a plant growing 6 to 12 feet tall. The slender, lance-shaped leaves grow 4 to 10 inches long on a stalk that has short, stiff hairs. Several flower heads grow on a single stalk; they are 2 to 3 inches wide and look like mini sunflowers, except that the center disks are yellow instead of black and are smaller. As the rhizomes develop, they eventually

Jerusalem artichoke has a bold yellow blossom.

grow into a tuber. The tubers are lumpy, 2 to 5 inches long, with smooth skin and crisp, white flesh. The plant spreads by its tubers, not seeds.

The wild Jerusalem artichoke grows like crazy just like the cultivated variety. If you plant the cultivated variety, some will invariably escape. I often find big colonies of Jerusalem artichokes in sunny fields.

Where and When to Gather

Jerusalem artichoke grows in river floodplains, along small creeks and lakes, and in sunny, wet areas. It prefers a sandy loam. Gather the tubers in the late fall, winter, or early spring. Do not dig them up before late November. The cold weather makes the tubers convert their inulin to simple sugars, making them sweeter. If you eat them before they are ripe, they can give you a bad stomachache.

How to Eat

I first ate Jerusalem artichokes in a restaurant in Chicago where I worked. We took the tubers and sliced them, dipped them in a tempura batter, and deep-fried them. They can be used as a vegetable in soup or can be roasted. Be sure to cook them, so you can digest them without any problem.

How to Preserve

Keep the tubers in an airtight container in a refrigerator or in moist sand in a root cellar.

Future Harvests

Jerusalem artichoke is considered to be invasive. In the wild, you can find big colonies. Thinning them out by digging some up actually helps the plants thrive.

Warning

Consuming raw wild Jerusalem artichoke tubers can give you a bad stomachache.

juneberry

Amelanchier species
serviceberry

EDIBLE fruit

Juneberries really do ripen in June. As soon as you see them ripen, collect them, because birds and other critters will devour them for their sweet pulp and almond-flavored, crunchy seeds.

How to Identify

Juneberry is a shrub or small tree. Its white flowers, which grow in a long cluster, have five straplike petals and many stamens in the center. The flowers appear before the leaves but often are still blooming when the leaves begin to unfurl. The trees put on quite a beautiful display when they are in bloom. The alternate, oval to elliptic, finely toothed leaves have thin leafstalks and turn a pretty amber color in autumn. Juneberry bark is gray and usually very smooth, although on older trees it may develop shallow grooves. Juneberry

Both ripe and slightly unripe berries adorn this juneberry tree.

fruit looks like blueberries growing on a tree. They are about the same size and shape, and like blueberries, have a five-pointed crown at the flower end. That crown is an important identification feature of juneberries. The juicy berries turn from green to red and finally dark purple when ripe.

Where and When to Gather

Juneberries grow in full to partial sunlight in lakesides, woodlands, and parks. Because of their attractive early spring flowers and beautiful fall foliage, they are frequently planted as ornamentals.

Gather juneberries in late spring to early summer. Because all the fruit doesn't ripen simultaneously, you can come back repeatedly and extend the harvest over several weeks. You can gather the slightly unripe berries as well as the ripe ones.

How to Gather

Juneberries are easy to collect by hand. You can also lay down a dropcloth and shake the tree gently. When fully ripe, juneberries are very fragile, so do not pile them up too much in a container. Do not use a bag, or they will become smashed.

How to Eat

You can eat juneberries seeds and all. The juicy pulp of juneberries is mild and slightly sweet, but what makes this wild fruit so great is the combination of its juiciness with the subtle almond flavor of its tiny, soft seeds, which is more pronounced in the slightly unripe fruit. The seeds in the unripe fruit also have a pleasant chewiness to them.

Juneberries make great pie. They are also good fresh combined with strawberries, which are in season at approximately the same time. They contain quite a bit of pectin and make good jam. You can also add them to muffins, quick breads, and pancakes. They make fabulous sorbet and ice cream. Just imagine juneberry ice cream with chunky, chewy bits of almond-flavored seeds!

How to Preserve

Like most berries, juneberries freeze well. You can also dry them or make a vinegar from them.

Future Harvests

There is no need to limit your harvest. It is nearly impossible to gather all of them.

juniper

Juniperus species

EDIBLE berries, needles

Juniper is an evergreen shrub or tree native to North America. The berries can be used in cooking and to make gin. The fresh berries taste piney, citrusy, and green. When dried, they have a clean, sharp flavor.

The berries of juniper smell like gin when crushed.

How to Identify

Juniper is a small tree or shrub growing from 2 to 20 feet tall. It has thin, soft, fragrant bark and hollow, spiky needles up to ½ inch long. Small yellow flowers appear in May or June. The fruits are green and turn into a type of cone that takes years to produce a juniper berry. The berries are dark blue when ripe. Only female trees produce berries.

Where and When to Gather

Juniper grows in poor, rocky, mountainous soil. The berries start to ripen in November and persist into winter.

How to Gather

The best way to gather the berries is by picking them off the tree, or you can lay a dropcloth on the ground and hit the branches to loosen the berries.

How to Eat

Juniper berries can be eaten fresh or dried. The dried berries are a classic ingredient in French game dishes in the fall and winter. You can use dried, ground berries instead of black pepper. And the dried berries can be used to make your own gin or infused liqueur. The wood can be used to smoke seafood or pork.

How to Preserve

Keep the fresh berries in an airtight container in the refrigerator. They will last a long time. Dried berries will last indefinitely.

Future Harvests

There is no need to limit your harvest of juniper berries.

Warning

Juniper should just be used as a seasoning or flavoring for food or drinks. There are varying reports that if ingested in large quantities, it can be toxic.

kousa dogwood

Cornus kousa

EDIBLE fruit

Landscapers love to plant this tree for its graceful beauty, and I love to eat the fruit for its sweet, persimmonlike pulp.

How to Identify

Kousa dogwood is a small Asian tree that grows up to 30 feet tall, and has mottled brown bark. Its coarsely toothed, elliptical, opposite leaves grow 4 inches long. The flowers look similar to other dogwood blooms in that they have four white bracts that look like petals, but the bracts are pointed rather than rounded. Also, kousa dogwood has a small, green ball in the middle of the flower, which becomes the fruit in May. The fruit is warty, globular, and pink to red, and softens as it ripens.

Where and When to Gather

Landscapers love to plant this tree in parks, botanical gardens, and in people's yards. Gather the fruit September through October. The quality of the fruit can vary from tree to tree.

The fruit of the kousa dogwood should be peeled to enjoy the pulp.

Kousa dogwood in bloom is a spectacular sight.

How to Gather
Gather the fruit by plucking them off the tree or picking them up off the ground.

How to Eat
Kousa dogwood fruit is best eaten raw. Cooking destroys the flavor. Most people cannot agree on what it tastes like. Some say the flavor is like apple with the texture of ripe persimmon, while others say it is like a combination of mango and apricot. Use the fruit to make jellies, desserts, and savory dishes. The skin is unpleasantly bitter.

How to Preserve
Keep the fruit in an airtight container in a refrigerator for up to one week.

Future Harvests
There is no need to limit your harvest of the fruit.

kudzu

Pueraria montana var. *lobata*

EDIBLE young leaves, flowers, roots

Have you ever been walking in the woods in August and smelled something grapelike and floral? Chances are, you smelled kudzu blooming. Kudzu, in the pea family, was originally brought to America from Japan, where they cultivate it for the root. The powdered root will thicken liquids so they are clear, not cloudy like with wheat flour. The young leaves taste like bland spinach.

Kudzu has grape-scented flowers.

How to Identify

Kudzu is a semi-woody perennial vine that climbs up to 100 feet and sprawls all over the place. Its three alternate, ovate leaves are 4 to 6 inches long. The flowers, which are pealike and purple, grow 4 to 8 inches long and smell like grapes. The large tuberous roots look like gigantic sweet potatoes and grow for miles underground.

Where and When to Gather

Kudzu grows in fields, woods, and along roads. It lies dormant during the winter, sprouts out in late spring, and grows through the summer. Gather the young leaves in late spring before they get tough. The flowers bloom in August and last for a couple of weeks. The roots are best in the fall and winter.

How to Gather

The leaves and flowers grow attached to the vine by a thin stem. Use scissors to cut the flowers and leaves from the vine. Use a shovel to dig up the roots.

How to Eat

The young leaves have a bland flavor, but are excellent as a green in place of spinach in quiches and lasagna. You can also fry them like potato chips. The flowers are my favorite part of the plant. They have a strong grapey, floral fragrance. The best way to capture that fragrance is by making jelly. Peel the roots before using, because the skin will lend an off flavor to foods. Once peeled, cut up the roots and grind them in a food processor to make a powder, which can be used just like cornstarch to thicken liquids.

How to Preserve

The young leaves and flowers should be stored with a damp paper towel on top in an airtight container in the refrigerator. Store kudzu powder in an airtight container in a dark cupboard at room temperature.

Future Harvests

There is no need to limit your harvest of kudzu. It is impossible to get rid of.

Warning

Kudzu is an extremely invasive plant that covers hillsides and the sides of roads throughout the South. It is frequently sprayed with herbicide, so use caution when picking. Never gather any part of kudzu from roadsides or any place where herbicide may have been sprayed.

lady's thumb

Polygonum persicaria
spotted lady's thumb

`EDIBLE` leaves

Along a popular running trail in a nearby park, there is lots of this often overlooked wild edible. The leaves have a pleasant, mild, green flavor and are tasty raw or cooked.

You can often find this invasive weed in parks and fields.

How to Identify

Lady's thumb is a branching annual plant up to 3½ feet high. Along its thin, sometimes reddish, wiry stems grow lance-shaped, alternate leaves that are 2 to 6 inches long and usually 1 inch or less wide, with smooth margins. The leaves sometimes have a faint dark spot in the center, supposedly looking as if a lady's thumb had bruised the leaf. The nodes where the leafstalks attach to the stems are wrapped in small sheaths tipped with hairs. The clusters of tiny pink flowers look like they will never open. They will not.

Where and When to Gather

Lady's thumb grows as a weed in gardens, parks, farmlands, and fields. It loves a combination of disturbed soil and full to partial sun. Collect lady's thumb leaves any time from mid-spring through early fall. Some patches of lady's thumb produce stronger-tasting leaves than others. Taste one before collecting more to see if you like the flavor.

How to Gather

Break off whole stems with the leaves attached. They will stay fresh longer if you keep them attached to the stems until ready to use. Then pinch off the tender leaves and discard the tough stems.

How to Eat

Lady's thumb leaves are good raw in salads. They can also be sautéed, steamed, or stir-fried. Because of their mild flavor, they are best mixed with other salad greens.

How to Preserve

Store the leaves with a damp paper towel on top in an airtight container in the refrigerator for up to a week.

Future Harvests

There is no need to limit your harvest.

lamb's quarters

Chenopodium album

goosefoot, fat hen

EDIBLE leaves, flowers, seeds

Ever notice a weed in your garden that has leaves with a silvery underside and water forms droplets on the leaves? That's lamb's quarters. Its nutty-tasting, young leaves can be eaten like spinach.

How to Identify

Lamb's quarters is an annual in the family Chenopodiaceae. The branching plant grows 3 to 5 feet tall and has rough diamond-shaped leaves. The underside of the leaves is silvery or white, which is a protective bloom. The bloom on the leaves makes water form droplets and run off. Just like when you wax your vehicle. Tiny green flowers grow in short, dense spikes at the plant's tips. By fall the flowers turn reddish brown.

Several edible plants are in the family Chenopodiaceae. They are all odorless. Orache (*Atriplex patula*) is salty-tasting and grows near seashores. Its leaves are

This common weed has leaves that taste like spinach, but stronger.

arrowhead-shaped. Strawberry blite (*Chenopodium capitatum*) has triangular leaves and tasteless red fruits.

Where and When to Gather

Lamb's quarters comes up in gardens, backyards, and sunny, disturbed soil. Start looking for it in early March. By May, it is tough and starting to bolt.

How to Gather

The young leaves, flowers, and reddish brown seeds are edible. Clip or pinch off the young leaves and flowers. To use the seeds, gather them and then winnow them (see Winnowing Seeds and Grain, page 18).

How to Eat

The young leaves can be eaten raw or cooked. They taste nutty, and the appealing nuttiness comes out even more when you have cooked them. Use the leaves like you would spinach. The flowers are best eaten raw. The seeds are perfect in breads, soups, and casseroles.

How to Preserve

Store the leaves in an airtight container in a cool, dark place like a cupboard. The seeds can be milled into flour. Once milled, the flour should be stored in the freezer.

Future Harvests

To ensure a harvest year after year, do not take everything.

Warning

Be careful where you pick lamb's quarters. The roots of the plant can pull potentially toxic contaminants from the soil, and the plant then traps and stores the toxins in its cells.

Loomis's mountain mint

Pycnanthemum loomisii

EDIBLE leaves

This tall, striking mint plant grows up to 3 feet tall, has smooth leaves that develop a white tinge, and the leaves have a strong menthol flavor.

How to Identify

Loomis's mountain mint is in the mint family. It is a loosely branched plant that grows 12 to 36 inches tall. Its green, oval leaves are 1 to 2 inches long with toothed margins. The leaves develop a distinctive, white powderlike surface by midsummer. The white or purple-spotted flowers have four stamens and are borne in clusters that are 1 inch across. The seeds are tiny and smooth.

During the summer, a distinctive white bloom develops on the leaves of Loomis's mountain mint.

Where and When to Gather

Loomis's mountain mint grows in open fields, along roadsides, and at the edge of woods. It appears in May, and then grows all summer and into October. Gather the leaves at any time during the summer.

How to Gather

Gather the leaves by cutting the stem with the leaves still attached. Do not gather Loomis's mountain mint in the heat of the day, because the leaves are delicate and will wilt.

How to Eat

Loomis's mountain mint can be used raw or cooked. It is nice to chew on it raw because it freshens your breath. If you cook with it, use it to balance sweet things like strawberries and honeysuckle infusions.

How to Preserve

Store Loomis's mountain mint with a damp paper towel on top in an airtight container in the refrigerator.

Future Harvests

Do not harvest a lot at one time from a single plant. Even in the best weather conditions, the plant is slow to regenerate.

marsh marigold

Caltha palustris

cowslip

EDIBLE young leaves, flower buds, stalks

Marsh marigold comes along in late winter when you are craving fresh greens. This plant also provides tasty flower buds that can be pickled like capers.

How to Identify

Marsh marigold is a perennial growing up to 24 inches tall. It has numerous, green, glossy leaves with rounded blades up to 6 inches across that grow on long stalks from the base of the plant. When mature, the leaves are ruffled. The flowers are bright yellow with five to nine sepals that look like 1-inch-wide petals and hang in clusters. The flowers produce starlike fruits with red seeds.

Marsh marigold's young leaves are some of the first edible greens in early spring.

Where and When to Gather

Marsh marigold grows in swamps, marshes, and wet areas in shade or part shade but rarely in full sun. Gather the young leaves and stalks in March when the plant is only 3 to 7 inches high and before any flowers have opened. Flower buds should also be gathered in March before the flowers open.

How to Gather

Cut the young leaves off at the leafstalk with shears. Gather the stalks the same way, and remove the dirty, papery sheath at the base of the stalk. Use your hands to pinch off the unopened flower buds.

How to Eat

Marsh marigold leaves must be cooked. When raw, they are acrid and should not be eaten. Boil the leaves in several changes of fresh water. I boil them three times, the last time for twenty minutes. After cooking, they become mushy. Purée the cooked greens and use in a cream-based sauce. My favorite part of this plant is the unopened flower buds. They are excellent pickled like capers.

How to Preserve

Pickle the unopened flower buds like you would a caper.

Future Harvests

There is no need to limit your harvest.

Warning

The raw greens contain protoanemonin, which is poisonous. The cooking process removes it.

mayapple

Podophyllum peltatum

`EDIBLE` fruit

This distinctive plant produces a single, delicious, tropical-tasting fruit.

How to Identify

Mayapple is a 1-foot-tall forest perennial. It grows in a Y-shape, with two large, spreading, umbrellalike leaves growing on stems that attach in the middle to a central stem. A single flower 2 inches across, with six to nine white petals and yellow pistils and stamens, grows where the two stems meet. The egg-shaped green fruit is about the size of a lemon and turns yellow when ripe. The flower appears in May, and the "apple" (the fruit) is ripe in late summer.

Mayapple plants usually grow in colonies.

Where and When to Gather

Mayapples grow in groups in moist, open woods. Collect only ripe mayapples in late summer, because the green unripe ones are toxic. The fruit is challenging to collect because not every plant produces fruit, some years are better than others, and animals usually gobble them up first.

How to Gather

Gather ripe mayapples by plucking them off the plant or by finding them on the ground after a storm. You can pick them when they are almost ripe and ripen them indoors, but the ones that ripen on the plant are best.

How to Eat

Mayapple has an intoxicating, tropical scent with a flavor that is similar to guava or passion fruit. The fragrance is what attracts critters. Discard the skin and seeds because they are unpleasantly bitter. The pulp makes a fantastic jam if you can collect enough.

How to Preserve

Store mayapples in an airtight container in the refrigerator for up to one week. One easy way to preserve the fruit for use later is to separate the pulp from the seeds using a food mill, discard the seeds, and freeze the pulp in an ice cube tray.

Future Harvests

There is no need to limit your harvest. If you can collect them in any quantity, you are very lucky.

Warning

Only the pulp is edible. All other plant parts are toxic.

mayhaw

Crataegus aestivalis

eastern mayhaw, eastern May hawthorn

`EDIBLE` fruit

People go crazy over this southern delicacy in May. There are festivals celebrating its arrival. The tart, sweet, tropical-flavored fruit is considered by many to be one of the finest fruits for jelly.

How to Identify

Mayhaw is in the hawthorn family, which contains many different woody plants. It is a shrub or small tree growing up to 30 feet, and has sharply toothed, elliptical leaves that grow alternately on branches that have thorns and often zigzag. The flowers are symmetrical, pinkish white, and have five petals and five sepals that grow 2 to 3 inches wide. The fruit is small, red, and globe-shaped.

There is another type of mayhaw called western mayhaw (*Crataegus opaca*). It looks and tastes just like eastern mayhaw,

The fruit of the mayhaw bush is delicious.

but grows from Alabama to Texas. The biggest difference between mayhaw and the other species of hawthorn is that mayhaw fruit ripens in May whereas the fruit of the other species of hawthorn ripens in the fall.

Where and When to Gather

Mayhaw grows in bayous, low-lying wet areas, and wetlands in the Deep South. The fruit starts to ripen toward the end of April and is ready to pick in May.

How to Gather

Gather the fruit by just picking them off the tree. You may have to use a boat to pick them in some spots.

How to Eat

Mayhaw tastes like a tart apple with hints of mango, apricot, and pineapple. You can find many mayhaw recipes for jelly, but there are so many other things to do with this delicious fruit. The pulp can be used for jam, vinegar, and butters, while the juice could be turned into syrups, candy, and used in cocktails.

How to Preserve

The fruit should be kept in an airtight container in the refrigerator. Preserve the fruit for the fall and winter by turning it into vinegar, jams, and jellies.

Future Harvests

There is no need to limit your harvest of this southern delicacy.

maypop

Passiflora incarnata
passion flower, apricot vine

`EDIBLE` fruit

Maypop is a trailing vine that is known for its beautiful flower often called passion flower. You may come across it growing on an old fence or in a field. The fruit has a pulp that tastes like a tropical citrus fruit.

How to Identify

Maypop is a perennial climbing or trailing vine that grows 10 to 30 feet long. Its deeply lobed leaves grow alternately and are 3 to 5 inches long and wide. The unusual flowers have a ring of ten white sepals and petals underneath a burst of pink or purple threads, and in the center, there are five yellow anthers. The large, oval fruit grows 1 to 2½ inches long. The skin of the fruit starts out green, then turns yellow, and eventually orange. There are numerous flat, dark seeds in the yellowish pulp. Butterflies flock to this plant, which is one way to find it.

The maypop plant has a distinctive white and purple flower.

The egg-shaped fruits of maypop are yellow when ripe, orange when overripe.

Where and When to Gather

Maypop grows in old fields and climbs along fences. Start looking for the ripe fruit in September, when the skin gets wrinkled. My favorites are the ones with yellow skin, before they turn orange.

How to Gather

Gather maypops by plucking them off the vine. Sometimes after a storm, they will get knocked to the ground, and those are usually ripe.

How to Eat

The part of the fruit that you eat is the pulp around the seeds. Using your hands, break open the fruit and scoop out the pulp. The peel is not edible. You can eat the seeds, but they have a bitter grittiness to them. Try the pulp at different stages of ripeness. When the fruits are just ripe, they have a sourness to them, and when they are really ripe, they taste sour, sweet, and tropical. They really taste like nothing else.

How to Preserve

Keep the pulp with the seeds in an airtight container in the refrigerator.

Future Harvests

Some of the fruits invariably become destroyed after heavy storms. So, it is near impossible to collect all of them. You can also help the plant self-seed by spitting out the seeds after snacking on some of the fruits while foraging.

milkweed

Asclepias syriaca

EDIBLE seedpods, seeds, young shoots, flowers

Milkweed is an attractive native plant that feeds monarch butterflies, and also gives us several edibles, from the seedpods to the young shoots.

How to Identify

Milkweed first appears in spring as slender, unbranched shoots not more than ½ inch thick with a few untoothed, fuzzy, oval leaves at the tip. If you snap off a piece of a shoot, a milky white latex oozes out.

As milkweed continues to grow, its single green stalks reach 3 to 6 feet tall without branching. The opposite leaves that attach to the stem in pairs on the older plants are 4 to 9 inches long and half as wide, with an oblong, smooth-edged shape.

Milkweed has pom-pomlike blooms.

After flowering, milkweed produces edible seedpods.

Milkweed flowers start out looking like miniature broccoli heads. They appear on the top 1 to 2 feet of the plants in the leaf axils. Eventually they open up into round, pinkish purple flower heads with numerous florets. The flowers are white and produce seedpods that look otherworldly: they are characteristically sickle-shaped, pointed at one tip, look somewhat like okra, and usually have a warty surface. The mature pods, which grow 2 to 5 inches long, are filled with a gossamer fluff.

Where and When to Gather
Milkweed prefers sunny, open fields. Collect the shoots from mid- to late spring when they are no more than a foot or so high and the stems are still tender enough to snap easily. Collect the flowers in June and July while they are still fully green and look like miniature broccoli florets. Collect the pods and their white innards before they have started to get fluffy in August.

How to Gather
Snap off the tender young shoots about 1 inch above soil level. Pinch or cut off the whole green flower heads. Cut off the very young seedpods while they are still very firm and less than 1½ inches long. Open up the pods to pull out the milkweed "cheese" when they are just starting to lose their firmness but are still green.

How to Eat

The shoots are good simply boiled for fifteen to twenty minutes. Once cooked, try adding them to frittatas or casseroles, or simply eating them as is with a little seasoning. Milkweed's green flower heads can be boiled, stir-fried, steamed, or added to soups.

Use your hands or a knife to open the firm milkweed pods with their moist but not fluffy white filling that is the future seeds. Scoop out the moist white substance and discard the outer casing. Boil it and then use it in anything that calls for cheese. The texture is like cheese and is my favorite part of the plant. Use it in any recipe where you want a cheeselike texture.

How to Preserve

Milkweed shoots, immature flower heads, and very young seedpods are best preserved by blanching and then freezing them. They are also excellent pickled.

Future Harvests

Leave some of the flowers and seedpods on the milkweed plants so the plant can regenerate.

Warning

When milkweed appears in spring as slender, unbranched shoots, another plant comes up at the same time, dogbane or *Apocynum cannabinum*, which is poisonous and looks very similar and also leaks white latex. The key to safely identifying milkweed shoots is to remember that milkweed is covered with velvety hairs, whereas dogbane is hairless. Just past the shoot stage, you can easily tell the difference. Dogbane branches as it matures and the stems develop a reddish color, whereas milkweed continues to grow in single green stalks 3 to 6 feet tall, rarely if ever branching.

Milkweed doesn't agree with a small percentage of people, causing them to vomit. Try a small amount first. Also, milkweed is not bitter. If your taste buds detect any bitterness, you've got the wrong plant.

mulberry

Morus rubra
black mulberry, red mulberry
`EDIBLE` fruit

Mulberry trees are often planted in yards to attract birds. They also grow wild along forest edges and open fields. The fruit has a distinctive taste, somewhat like blackberries but different.

How to Identify

Mulberry is a deciduous tree 60 to 70 feet tall with rough, reddish bark. Its oval, toothed, alternate leaves grow on slender, zigzag, yellowish brown twigs. Male and female flowers, which are green and tiny, grow on the same tree. The fruits are cylindrical; they start out whitish green and then turn red, then black when ripe. They grow 1 to 2 inches long.

Another mulberry species, white mulberry (*Morus alba*), is less commonly

The fruit of the mulberry tree turns black when ripe.

found in the Southeast. It is similar in appearance and growth, but some cultivars have berries that are white, not black, when ripe.

Where and When to Gather

Mulberries usually are ripe starting in May and lasting into June. Mulberries grow in open woods, along field edges, in parks, and along streets.

How to Gather

Mulberry fruit is often knocked to the ground by wind or rain. Pick the berries up off the ground and carefully place them in a bucket or lay down a dropcloth and shake a branch. When using a bucket, make sure not to pile them up too high because the delicate fruit can become bruised.

How to Eat

Use mulberries in any way you would use a blackberry. They dry really well, which gives the fruit an interesting, chewy texture.

How to Preserve

Keep mulberries in an airtight container in the refrigerator for up to one week. Dried mulberries will keep for up to six months in an airtight container.

Future Harvests

There is no need to limit your harvest.

New Jersey tea

Ceanothus americanus

EDIBLE leaves

New Jersey tea is an unassuming plant that grows in open fields. When I first learned about this plant, it blew my mind that a wild tea plant grew here in the South. The leaves of New Jersey tea make a refreshing beverage that tastes like black tea.

How to Identify

New Jersey tea is a small, low shrub growing up to 3 feet tall. Its oval, dark green leaves grow 1½ to 3 inches long and are finely toothed on the edges. If you look closely at the leaves, you will notice there are several veins on each side of the midvein curving toward the edge of the leaf. The tiny, white flowers have five petals and grow at the tips of the branches.

The tea made from this plant was popular during the Revolutionary War because

New Jersey tea shrubs grow wild in our region.

English tea was boycotted. It was supplied from the Pine Barrens of New Jersey, hence the name.

Where and When to Gather

New Jersey tea grows in sandy, rocky soils in open fields, along roadsides, and in waste areas. You can gather the leaves any time, but the flavor is the best when the plant blooms, beginning in early July.

How to Gather

Gather the leaves by clipping the stem.

How to Eat

The dried or fresh leaves of New Jersey tea make an excellent tea. The longer you steep the leaves, the stronger the tea will be. Once you have made the tea, think about using the liquid in other ways, such as for syrups and for poaching seafood.

How to Preserve

If you are going to use the fresh leaves, I recommend using them straightaway or storing them in a refrigerator in an airtight container with a damp paper towel over them for just a few days. To dry them, use a dehydrator or hang them upside down on the branch in a dry, well-ventilated area until dry. Then store the dry leaves in an airtight container.

Future Harvests

New Jersey tea is a hardy perennial, but never take all of it. Harvest it sparingly.

oak

Quercus species

`EDIBLE` nuts (acorns)

Oak trees produce many acorns, a traditional food source for Native Americans. It is labor-intensive to process acorns, but once leached of their tannins, they taste like chestnuts.

How to Identify

Numerous oak species grow in the Southeast. They have several identifying characteristics in common. Oak leaves are alternate, leathery, and usually but not always lobed. The leaves of white oak (*Quercus alba*) have rounded lobes, whereas those in the red and black oak group (*Q. falcata* and *Q. velutina*) have sharply pointed lobes.

Some oaks have unlobed, toothed, hollylike leaves. Oak's male and female flowers look like dangling, yellow-green, lumpy threads. The acorns are nuts that have various shapes: some are shaped like 2-inch-long, ½-inch-wide bullets, some are round and 1 inch or more in diameter, and some are small and squat. All acorns have thin, brown shells and sit in a detachable cup.

The bark of white oak (*Quercus alba*) peels off in strips.

These acorns are from a few of the red and white oak species.

Where and When to Gather

Oaks grow in many different kinds of habitat, from floodplains to ridges and mixed hardwood forests. Gather acorns as soon as they start falling to the ground in late summer and fall. The trees do not produce the nuts consistently every year. Some years it's easy to collect a large amount quickly, while other years the nuts are scarce. You want to rescue your acorns from the ground before the bugs or squirrels get to them, so don't wait too long to gather.

How to Gather

Before gathering acorns, check each for a pinhole in the shell, which means it is wormy. Other signs that an acorn is not food-worthy are a strongly attached cap and a shell that is whitish rather than brown. To eliminate any buggy acorns that may have made it into your collection bag, put them in a big bowl of water. The good acorns will sink to the bottom. Discard any floaters.

How to Eat

Acorns must be leached to remove their mouth-drying tannins before they can be eaten. The following two methods both work, but with significantly different results:

Hot water processing Remove the thin shells by cutting the acorn in half with a knife or a light hammer tap. Put the shelled acorns in a pot, cover them with water, and bring to a boil. The water will turn brownish from the tannins leaching out of the acorns. Drain, return the acorns to the pot, cover with clean water, and repeat. It speeds things up if you have a second pot of water coming to a boil soon after the first pot. Continue boiling the acorns in fresh changes of water until the water no longer turns brownish. Taste a nut to see if it has been leached long enough. It should taste like a chestnut without a bitter taste.

Cold water processing Shell and grind the nutmeats. I like to use a food processor for grinding. Once ground, leach by stirring the acorn meal together with cold water in the biggest pot you've got. Leave overnight, then strain through cheesecloth. Repeat until the acorn meal no longer has any bitter flavor when you taste it.

Hot water–processed acorns can be shelled and eaten as is, or ground into meal in a food processor. You can then spread the ground acorn meal on baking sheets and dry it in an oven on low heat. Use the dried meal in oatmeal, porridges, and baked goods, or regrind it into a fine flour. Hot water–processed acorn flour is dark and gives baked goods a crumbly consistency. I usually combine it with wheat or other flours. Acorns do not have gluten, so don't use more than 25 percent acorn flour to other flour in a dough.

Cold water–processed acorn flour is lighter colored and although it, too, is gluten free, it produces a spongy texture in baked goods that is closer to a wheat-flour texture than anything you can get with hot water–leached acorn flour. You can use 100 percent cold water–processed acorn flour in quick breads made with baking soda or baking powder. Acorn flour makes excellent pasta as well. My favorite thing to do with acorn flour is to make biscuits, griddle cakes, and hoecakes.

How to Preserve

Store acorns leached by either method or acorn flour in the freezer. If you do not store acorns in the freezer, they will go rancid quickly.

Future Harvests

There is no need to limit your harvest. But leave some for the birds and other animals.

oxeye daisy

Chrysanthemum leucanthemum

EDIBLE leaves, young stems, unopened flower buds

The oxeye daisy is notable for its leaves, which have a unique, sweet chewiness.

How to Identify

Oxeye daisy is a perennial herb that grows in a basal rosette of green leaves 2 to 6 inches long that are irregularly toothed, becoming smaller the higher up the stem. The stem grows 14 to 30 inches tall and is unbranched. Leaves will grow alternately along the stem. The flowers at the tips of the stems are flat, yellow disks with white petals.

Where and When to Gather

Oxeye daisy grows in open fields, roadsides, and disturbed soil. The leaves and

The blooms of oxeye daisy are classic daisy flowers in shape and color.

Oxeye daisies rise above their compact leaves by midsummer.

young stems are at their best from May into June. Gather the flower buds in mid to late May. Once the flower blooms and dies, the flavor of the leaves becomes bitter.

How to Gather
Gather leaves, stems, and flower buds by clipping them.

How to Eat
The flavor of oxeye daisy leaves is really unique. It has a chewy sweetness that is complex and reminds you of a lot of flavors. The leaves are best used raw. Use them in salads or as a garnish. The unopened flower buds can be pickled like capers. The stems can be lightly steamed or you can try fermenting them. Fermenting is a part of the pickling process. This step in pickling produces lactic acid, which helps preserve the product and is also a natural probiotic that aids the digestion process. You do not have to pickle something you ferment. Beer is fermented but not pickled.

How to Preserve
To preserve freshness for all the edible parts of oxeye daisy, keep them with a damp paper towel on top in an airtight container in the refrigerator.

Future Harvests
Only take some of the leaves. Once the flower starts to bloom, harvest sparingly.

pawpaw

Asimina triloba
custard apple
EDIBLE fruit

Pawpaw bears the largest fruit growing wild in the United States. It is shaped like a mango, has a custard texture, and tastes like a combination of banana, mango, and pear.

How to Identify

Pawpaw is a tree that grows no more than 25 feet high. Its smooth, toothless, drooping leaves are 6 to 12 inches long on light brown twigs. It produces maroon, bell-shaped flowers. When ripe, the mango-shaped fruit has creamy flesh and multiple, large seeds.

Another type of pawpaw, called dwarf pawpaw (*Asimina parviflora*), grows more like a shrub up to 15 feet high. The fruit is the same, but smaller.

Where and When to Gather

Pawpaw grows in moist, fertile soil along riverbanks, streams, floodplains, and occasionally in the understory of the forest. Start looking for ripe, yellow pawpaw fruit in August.

How to Gather

Pawpaw fruit is often knocked to the ground by storms. You can also just pluck them off the tree.

How to Eat

You can eat the flesh raw or use it in just about any dessert or savory dish. The seeds inside the fruit are not edible.

How to Preserve

Store the pulp of the fruit in an airtight container in a refrigerator. The whole fruit should be kept in a cool, dry place or in a refrigerator.

Future Harvests

It can be difficult to find ripe, wild pawpaw. There is no need to limit your harvest.

Warning

Be cautious eating pawpaw the first time because it does not agree with everyone. Also, never eat the unripe fruit, because it will make you vomit.

The pawpaw tree has green oblong leaves.

Pawpaw fruit has a custard texture.

pennywort

Hydrocotyle bonariensis

EDIBLE leaves, stems

When I walk onto the beach here in the Southeast, I frequently run across pennywort. The succulent leaves have a unique, sweet flavor and the stems have a parsleylike tang.

Pennywort grows at the edge of the beach where dunes start.

How to Identify

Pennywort is usually 6 to 10 inches tall. Its thick, succulent, round leaves are bluntly toothed and grow up to 2 inches wide. The long stalks are attached to the center of the leaf. The white or greenish flowers are borne on separate stalks.

Where and When to Gather

Pennywort grows on dune swales, salt marsh edges, and the upper edges of the beach. The best time to gather pennywort is March through May.

How to Gather

Gather pennywort by using scissors to snip the stems.

How to Eat

I love the texture and unusual flavor of pennywort. It is traditionally used in Asian cooking in salads, stir-fries, tea, and Asian soft drinks like Gotu Kola. Beverages made from the leaves and stems have a refreshing quality. The leaves and stems can be used raw or lightly cooked. I like to eat pennywort raw so that the succulent texture of the leaves and crunch of the stems are left intact. If you are using pennywort in a stir-fry, put it in at the end so it can retain its crunchiness.

How to Preserve

Keep pennywort with a damp paper towel over it in an airtight container in the refrigerator. The stems have a delicious tang that would be tasty when lightly pickled.

Future Harvests

Cut pennywort to keep it regrowing for a long, bountiful harvest, and so it will come back year after year.

pickerelweed

Pontederia cordata

EDIBLE young leaves, seeds

Pickerelweed grows in wetlands and has edible young leaves and seeds. The leaves taste like other cooked greens, and the seeds have a nutty flavor.

How to Identify

Pickerelweed leaves usually have an arrowlike shape but sometimes lack the back end of the arrow, so they are more lance-shaped or like narrow triangles. The leaves can get as big as 9 inches long and 5 inches wide, and grow in a rosette or a loose clump.

Two other plants with arrowlike leaves that like the same wetland habitat and often grow alongside pickerelweed are wapato or arrowhead (see page 243), and arrow arum (*Peltandra virginica*), which is only very marginally edible. Both these plants have pointed back lobes on the leaves, whereas pickerelweed's are more

Pickerelweed has beautiful bluish purple blooms.

rounded. Wapato leaves have a central midvein that pickerelweed and arrow arum lack.

Pickerelweed's hollow flower stalks shoot up from the center of the leaf rosettes and grow 2 to 3 feet tall. The individual flowers are a pretty lavender-blue and clustered on the top few inches of the flower stalk in a bottlebrushlike flower head. Each flower opens from the bottom up, so that often the tip of the flower head looks bald compared to the colorful lower portion. Just below the flower head, the flower stalk is wrapped in a sheath. The fruit are small oval capsules, each containing a single seed.

Where and When to Gather

Pickerelweed grows in very wet soil, usually in shallow, slow-moving freshwater. You'll find it at the edges of ponds and lakes, and in marshes and bogs.

Pickerelweed's showy flowers bloom from June to October. But come back earlier the following year to collect the leaves, either while they are still partially curled up like scrolls or very recently unfurled. Collect the seeds from August to November. As with any plant that grows in water, only harvest from unpolluted waters.

How to Gather

To gather pickerelweed, you need to be willing to get wet. Sometimes you can do it from a canoe, but the plant often grows close to the water's edge. Cut or snap off the very young leaves where they attach to the stems. Harvest the seeds by holding the stem in one hand while you strip off the seed capsules with the other hand. I do this directly into a collection bag I have tied to a belt loop on my pants.

How to Eat

The greens are good raw in salads, lightly steamed, or stir-fried. The raw seeds lend a crunchy texture to salads. The dried seeds can also be cooked for cereal using a ratio of 2:1 (seeds to grain). You can also grind the dried seeds into a nut-flavored flour that is good combined with grain flours for making baked goods. Toast the seeds before grinding to enhance the flavor.

How to Preserve

Dried pickerelweed seeds keep for over a year. The greens should be stored with a damp paper towel on top in an airtight container in the refrigerator.

Future Harvests

Only pick a few leaves from each plant. Pickerelweed spreads by a network of rhizomes. New plants will generate from those rhizomes, even though you cut off some of the edible leaves.

pineapple weed

Matricaria matricarioides

EDIBLE leaves, flowers

You may think upon seeing this plant for the first time that it is chamomile. You will definitely know that it is not when you bruise the leaves with your hands and smell the fragrance of pineapple. The flowers and leaves, when infused in water, make a tasty, aromatic tea.

How to Identify

Pineapple weed does look similar to chamomile, but the pineapplelike aroma sets it apart. It can grow up to 1½ feet tall, but it's usually smaller, even as short as 2 inches high. Its leaves are very finely dissected, which gives them a feathery appearance and feel. Pineapple weed flower heads look like ¼- to ½-inch yellow-green balls or rounded cones, each made up of many tiny

When you crush the leaves of pineapple weed, they really do smell like pineapple.

flowers. If you squish a pineapple weed flower head, it breaks apart into the individual flowers. Unlike chamomile, pineapple weed doesn't have white petal-like ray flowers.

The whole plant is aromatic when crushed, with a scent like a cross between chamomile and pineapple. The aroma is an important identifying characteristic.

Where and When to Gather

Pineapple weed grows in full sun in open fields, lawns, driveways, and roadsides. Gather it while it is flowering, from July to October.

How to Gather

Gather the top few inches of the plant to use in tea by pinching off or cutting off with scissors.

How to Eat

I like pineapple weed best as a tea. Use the flowers and leaves by pouring boiling hot water over fresh or dried pineapple weed. Cover with a lid and let steep for five to ten minutes, then strain. Once you've brewed your tea, you can chill it to make a refreshing beverage on a hot summer day. I also like to poach seafood, especially shrimp and scallops, in pineapple weed tea. Once you have made the tea, use the liquid to make a simple syrup for use in cocktails or to make sorbet. Pineapple weed also makes wonderful sorbet.

How to Preserve

Dried pineapple weed keeps its flavor for at least six months if stored away from direct light or heat. I've also had good results with pineapple weed syrup and pineapple weed–infused vodka.

Future Harvests

Pineapple weed quickly recovers after harvesting.

plantain

Plantago species

`EDIBLE` leaves, seed heads

This plant is not the one that bears the starchy fruit commonly eaten in Central and South America. I guarantee that you have walked past or mowed this plant in the yard a million times. It is very unassuming, but you might have noticed it once it goes to seed, because of the green, turning brown cone-shaped seed heads that taste like mushrooms.

How to Identify

There are two main *Plantago* species in the Southeast: common plantain (*P. major*) and English plantain (*P. lanceolata*). They grow as ground-hugging rosettes of smooth-edged leaves with prominent parallel veins. Common plantain has oval leaves that have smooth or gently toothed margins. English plantain has narrow leaves that grow up to a foot long and usually no more than 1 inch wide.

Plantain leaves have noticeable parallel veins. Break off a leaf anywhere along the base, and usually a few veins will stick out like white threads, somewhat like celery stalk threads.

The flowers and seeds grow on leafless stalks that emerge from the center of the leaf rosette. The flower heads may cover most of the stalk or just the top inch or so. Common plantain seed heads start out covered by green, scalelike seeds that eventually turn brown. English plantain has tiny white flowers projecting from the 1- to 2-inch seed heads.

Where and When to Gather

The best time to collect young, tender, nonstringy plantain leaves is in early spring to mid-spring, but you can harvest the younger leaves from spring through midsummer.

Collect the seed heads of common plantain when they are greenish brown. Also taste the seed heads at different times to find your favorite time to harvest. It's not really worth collecting English plantain seeds because the seed heads are small and the harvest is labor-intensive.

How to Gather

Pinch out the smallest leaves from the center of the leaf rosettes. Snap or cut off common plantain seed head stalks and dry them in cloth or paper bags before stripping the seeds off the stalks.

How to Eat

Young plantain leaves are a mild salad or cooked green, but are not my favorite part because of the stringiness of the leaves.

In the South, common plantain is a familiar volunteer in the yard.

My favorite part of this plant is the seed heads. I don't bother trying to separate the tiny seeds from the chaff. Just strip off the chaff-encased seeds and add them to muffins, breads, and other baked goods. I have also experimented with sautéing the whole seed head in butter with good results. I would imagine you could also make a mushroom-tasting infused oil with the seed heads. The seed heads really do taste like button or porcini mushrooms.

How to Preserve

Dried plantain seeds keep for at least a year. Simply store the seed heads in paper or cloth bags for two weeks, then strip the seeds off the stalk and store in airtight containers.

Future Harvests

Both types of plantain are incredibly invasive. Pick all you want.

pokeweed

Phytolacca americana
poke sallet, inkweed

`EDIBLE` young shoots

Have you ever heard the song "Poke Salad Annie" by Tony Joe White? Well, he's talking about pokeweed. Southerners have an almost mystical love for pokeweed, which is passed on from grandparents or other elderly relatives who wax on about their love for the greens. The young shoots taste like asparagus but stronger.

How to Identify

Pokeweed is a smooth, tall, branching herbaceous perennial that grows up to 10 feet tall with oval, long, smooth leaves 3 to 12 inches long and 2½ to 5 inches wide. The flowers are green and white with no true petals. Once the flowers bloom, they produce dark purple berries in late summer to early fall. The stems turn magenta.

Where and When to Gather

Pokeweed loves to grow in disturbed soil. It appears in early spring and grows until fall. The best time to gather young pokeweed shoots is in early spring.

These pokeweed shoots are perfect for harvesting.

Once the pokeweed plant is mature, it is not safe for eating.

How to Gather

The young shoots are the only edible part of the plant. Collect shoots when they are 6 to 8 inches tall or while still green. Shoots that are larger or that have turned magenta are poisonous. In fact, the whole plant is poisonous except for the young shoots.

How to Eat

Pokeweed must be boiled in two changes of water. After boiling, the shoots are safe to use. Pokeweed should never be bitter. If it is, you need to boil it more. Pokeweed works well as a side dish, in soups, in stews, and fried. A chef friend of mine loves to fry the green shoots whole and use them as an appetizer.

How to Preserve

Dry the cooked pokeweed shoots in a dehydrator or an oven set at a low temperature. You can then store them in ziplock bags and reconstitute them in soups or sauces.

Future Harvests

No need to limit your harvest of pokeweed. It has a long taproot, and once established is very hard to get rid of.

Warning

Again, the whole pokeweed plant is poisonous except for the young shoots. If you eat any other part, you will get severe vomiting, diarrhea, intestinal cramps, visual impairment, and weakened respiration. Death can occur. If you use pokeweed, be extremely careful.

prickly pear

Opuntia humifusa

eastern prickly pear, Indian fig, nopal

EDIBLE fruits, pads, seeds

Prickly pear is a cactus that produces padlike leaves called *nopales* in Mexico. The pads have a tangy, green pepper flavor with a hint of purslane and a mucilaginous texture like okra, and the fruits taste a bit like melon.

How to Identify

Prickly pear is a native cactus found in desertlike parts of North America, with fleshy, flattened, jointed green stems, or "pads," that are 2 to 4 inches wide and 4 to 6 inches long. The pads have small spines called glochids, and if you touch the spines, they can become embedded in your skin. The glochids are borne in clusters in pockets called areoles. The flowers of *Opuntia humifusa* are large and yellow, producing spiny, 1- to 2-inch-long fruits that are green and then turn reddish purple when ripe. The juicy flesh of the fruit has small, black, coarse seeds.

Where and When to Gather

Prickly pear grows principally in dry, sunny areas with sandy or rocky soil. Gather the young pads in May and the fruits in September.

How to Gather

Always wear heavy gloves when picking the pads and fruits from prickly pear. The glochids act as the plant's defense mechanism, and your skin will be quickly impaled if you do not protect it. The pads should be cut off with a knife so the plant can grow new pads. The fruit can be plucked off. Once you have picked the pads or fruit, you must clean off the glochids by scrubbing with a metal scrubbing tool, or you can remove them one by one using a knife. The pads have more glochids than the fruit. The seeds are gathered by straining the pulp through cheesecloth.

How to Eat

The pads can be cut up into strips or chunks and cooked in a lot of different ways. One common way to eat them is fried with eggs. You can eat the fruit pulp raw or cooked. The fruit must be peeled and the seeds strained before using the fruit. The pulp is delicious juiced and mixed with other beverages or just by itself. The coarse seeds can be eaten: dry and roast them, and then grind them into a flour and use in bread recipes.

The flowers of prickly pear will soon form fruits that are called *tunas* in Spanish.

The pads of prickly pear can be eaten.

How to Preserve

The pads will keep for at least a month in the refrigerator if you wrap them up so they do not dry out. The fruit will keep for months in an airtight container in the refrigerator.

Future Harvests

Do not take all the pads from a plant, but you can take all the fruit you want.

purple dead nettle

Lamium purpureum
red dead nettle

`EDIBLE` leaves, stems, flowers

Purple dead nettle catches your eye in January, when the plants, with their pinkish purple blooms, cover bare, open soil when everything is bleak and dreary. The earthy, mushroomlike flavor of the leaves and the crunchiness of the stems lend themselves to cooking.

How to identify

Purple dead nettle is a smallish, sprawling annual. It comes up in winter in lawns, gardens, pastures, and vacant lots. It is a small annual up to 16 inches tall, with triangular, heart-shaped leaves that clasp the square stem. The flowers are pinkish purple and tubular.

Purple dead nettle may be confused with henbit or ground ivy; all three plants are in the mint family, Lamiaceae. They look somewhat similar, but henbit has heart-shaped, jagged leaves, and purple dead nettle has triangular leaves that have fine hairs. Ground ivy does not get as tall as henbit and the leaves smell like mint,

The top of the purple dead nettle plant resembles a Japanese pagoda.

whereas henbit leaves do not. Purple dead nettle is more flavorful than henbit. While the foliage of purple dead nettle looks slightly like true nettle, the plant does not sting, and thus the name "dead nettle."

Where and When to Gather

Purple dead nettle grows in any ground that is bare or has been disturbed. It starts appearing after henbit in early winter and grows until late spring. You cannot ask for a more reliable plant.

How to Gather

Gather purple dead nettle from before to after it has bloomed. Harvest the flowers, leaves, and stems by cutting or breaking them off.

How to Eat

Use the young leaves and tops in salads. Purple dead nettle holds up well in cooking. The stems have a mild crunchiness to them. The ruffled leaves have a chewy texture. You will want to think of dishes that will bring out the mushroom-like flavor. Purple dead nettle has small, pinkish purple flowers that are edible but too small to use on their own, although they can be combined with the leaves.

How to Preserve

Purée and freeze the leaves and stems for sauces or make pesto with them. Store the young leaves with a damp paper towel on them in an airtight container in the refrigerator.

Future Harvests

There is no need to limit your harvest of purple dead nettle. It is not native to North America and is quite invasive. Once established, it is hard to get rid of.

purslane
Portulaca oleracea

EDIBLE leaves, stems

Purslane is often cultivated by farmers for chefs, who like to use the juicy, sour flavor of the succulent leaves in their dishes. I wonder if the farmers know they could probably just find this common, summer weed growing wild in their garden.

How to Identify

Purslane is a low-growing plant, no more than a few inches high, that spreads horizontally up to 2 feet across. It has thick, reddish, succulent stems with oval to spade-shaped leaves, ¼ to 1¼ inches long, that remind me of the leaves of a miniature jade plant. Its small yellow flowers have five petals, and the later oval seed capsules split around their middles to release many tiny black seeds.

Where and When to Gather

Purslane thrives in the warm to hot weather of late spring and summer of the Southeast. Look for it in sunny places

Purslane loves to come up in your garden during the summer.

with disturbed soil, especially in or near gardens, parks, and farmlands. Its succulent leaves and stems enable it to flourish even when summer droughts and heat have taken their toll on other leafy green edibles.

How to Gather

Use your hands or scissors to break off the juicy stems a few inches above the soil. All the aboveground parts of purslane are edible.

How to Eat

You can eat purslane leaves and stems raw or cooked. Raw, the plant has a juicy, slightly sour taste. It is good on its own or added to other salad ingredients. In Mexico, purslane is highly prized for making salsa. Cooked, purslane is slightly mucilaginous (I am not a big fan of cooked purslane). If you do cook it, add it at the end of making the dish so that the crunchy texture remains. Once the plant goes to seed, the thick stems become less tender, which makes them good for pickling.

How to Preserve

Store purslane in an airtight container with a damp paper towel on top in a refrigerator. The late, thick, tough stems make excellent pickles.

Future Harvests

Purslane self-seeds really well. There is no need to limit your harvest.

ramps

Allium tricoccum

wild leek, spring onion

EDIBLE leaves, stems, bulb ,seeds

Nothing makes people go crazier for wild edibles in the spring than ramps. Their strong, slightly garlicky, onion flavor is addictive.

How to Identify

Ramps are a perennial in the genus *Allium* (onion). They have smooth, waxy-looking green leaves with parallel veins. The leaves grow 2 to 3 inches wide and 8 to 10 inches long from a white stem. The bulb is small and white. The leaves start to die back in early summer, giving way to a cluster of small, six-petaled white flowers on top of a slender flower stalk. The seeds are small, black, and shiny.

There are many plants in the onion family that look like ramps. Remember: nothing that smells like onions is poisonous. Ramps always smell like onions.

The whole ramps plant can be eaten.

Ramps frequently can be found growing on the forest floor.

Where and When to Gather

Ramps grow in moist, rich woods in colonies. They start to appear in mid-spring and their season lasts till mid-May.

How to Gather

Gather ramps anytime in the spring before the leaves die back. Most people dig the whole plant up, but you can also just cut the plant off above ground.

How to Eat

The whole plant can be eaten. The strong garlic-onion flavor is more potent than that of a cultivated leek. Ramps can be sautéed, used in marinades, pickled, or turned into pesto. Ramps are good in just about anything.

How to Preserve

Pickled ramps are one of my favorite ways of eating them. It is also a great way to preserve them.

Future Harvests

Never take all the ramps you find. They take several years to regrow and in some places are becoming hard to find because of overharvesting.

red bay

Persea borbonia

swampbay, shorebay, tisswood

`EDIBLE` leaves

This small to tall evergreen tree grows near the beach all along the coastal plain in the Southeast. The leaves when crushed have a heavenly fragrance like lemon verbena.

How to identify

Red bay is in the laurel family, and is a shrub or short-trunked tree that grows 20 to 75 feet tall. It has thick, shiny, aromatic evergreen leaves with rust-colored hairs on the midvein underside. Densely hairy leafstalks grow from reddish brown bark. The small, yellow-green flowers are borne in clusters on hairy stalks, and produce small, dark blue to black, round berries from September to October.

This red bay shows its glossy leaves.

Where and When to Gather

You'll find red bay grows near the ocean beaches in our region. The leaves of red bay are evergreen, but I find the flavor is best during the warmer months.

How to Gather

Gather the leaves by plucking a few, or lop off a small branch of leaves. You do not need many leaves because they are very fragrant.

How to Eat

Red bay leaves have a citrusy, floral flavor. Use the leaves for infusions for making oils, syrups, liqueurs, and milk for ice cream. Red bay leaves can also be used with fish. They are versatile and can be used in sweet or savory dishes, as well as for mixed drinks.

How to Preserve

Red bay leaves can be infused into liqueurs, oils, syrups, or milk to make ice cream.

Future Harvests

Take just a few leaves here, a few there, from different trees. Do not strip the leaves off one tree.

redbud

Cercis canadensis

Judas tree

EDIBLE blooms

The redbud tree is one of the first trees to bloom in the late winter. The pretty purplish pink blooms cover the bare branches. The flowers, when not yet fully open, have a tasty green peanut flavor.

How to Identify

The redbud tree is in the pea family. It grows up to 40 feet tall with a small trunk and has toothless heart-shaped leaves that are 3 to 5 inches across. The pealike flowers are purplish pink. The fruit is a dark brown, flat pod 3 to 4 inches long.

Where and When to Gather

The redbud tree grows just about anywhere and it self-seeds well. Landscapers often use the tree in parks. The blooms start to appear in mid to late March and last for a few weeks.

The strong pink blossoms of the redbud tree are a harbinger of spring.

A redbud tree in full bloom is a beautiful sight.

How to Gather

Carefully pull the flowers directly from branches or cut branches you intend to take flowers from.

How to Eat

When redbud flowers are fully open, they do not taste like much. However, when they have not fully opened they have a green peanut flavor. Redbud flowers are tasty as a garnish, and they look intriguing in ice cubes for drinks.

How to Preserve

Pick the delicate redbud blooms early in the morning or late in the day. After picking them, store with a damp paper towel on them in an airtight container in the refrigerator.

Future Harvests

Always leave some flowers to mature. Otherwise the tree will soon die.

red clover

Trifolium pratense

`EDIBLE` flowers

Red clover is familiar to most of us, but I feel like the plant is passed by far too often in favor of more exciting wild edibles. The flowers have a mildly sweet flavor. There are many ways to use red clover beyond just food.

How to Identify

Red clover is a perennial found in much of the United States and Canada. Leaflets come in groupings of three and often sport a whitish, chevron-shaped mark. The leaflets and stalks are slightly hairy. The flowers look like pink or pinkish purple pom-poms composed of many individual florets. The whole flower head is ½ to 1¼ inches in diameter. The plants usually

Red clover blooms happily in spring and summer.

grow to about 16 inches tall but can look shorter because they sprawl.

Where and When to Gather

Red clover likes open, sunny areas and can often be found escaped from farm fields. Farmers often plant it as a cover crop because, like other plants in the family Fabaceae, red clover can fix atmospheric nitrogen in the soil and make it biologically available to other plants as a nutrient. It blooms prolifically in mid- to late spring or early summer, then slows down and will bloom sporadically depending on rainfall.

How to Gather

Look for fresh red clover flowers that are pink or pink tinged with purple, and without any trace of brown. Pinch off the blossoms along with a few leaves right at their base and place them into a container.

How to Eat

You can use red clover blossoms fresh or fully dried. The blossoms make an excellent tea with a mildly sweet flavor. Pour boiling water over the flowers, cover, and infuse for twenty to thirty minutes. Strain the blossoms out and serve hot or chilled. If you like your tea sweet like most Southerners, use honey instead of sugar.

The pom-pom–shaped flowers have a tough central core and base to which the tiny florets are attached. If you are going to use the flowers for eating, I recommend stripping the tender florets off the tough core and base. Use them, fresh or dried, in grain recipes such as rice, farro, or quinoa salads.

Dried, the florets can be used as a sort of flour to replace up to 25 percent of the wheat or other grain flour in recipes for baked goods. They add a lightly spongy texture, mild sweetness, and a dash of protein to whatever bread, muffin, or other baked good you are making. The easiest way to turn whole, dried red clover flowers into flour is to pulse them a few times in a food processor. The flour won't resemble grain flour, but will have a fluffy, soft texture. Remove any large, tough bits.

How to Preserve

Place whole red clover flowers and upper leaves in large paper or cloth bags, or between two fine-mesh screens, spread out in a more or less single layer. Leave in a dry place away from direct light or heat until the leaves are easy to crumble and the flowers are completely dry. Properly dried red clover turns from pink to a purplish hue, but is not brown.

Future Harvests

There is no need to limit your harvest.

rose

Rosa species

`EDIBLE` flowers, hips

Wild rose blossoms come in different shapes and colors, and are all fragrant and edible. The rose hips make nutritious jelly.

How to Identify

There are several different types of wild rose in the Southeast, including multiflora rose, pasture rose, and rugosa rose. Wild roses have edible fruit called "hips." The size of the flowers and hips vary from species to species.

Multiflora rose (*Rosa multiflora*) is a hardy perennial with climbing or trailing branches that form dense thickets. The flowers are white with five petals and protruding stamens. The leaves are alternate, feathery, and compound. Multiflora rose comes up along fences, woods, pastures,

The fragrant blooms of wild roses are perfect for candying.

and open fields. It flowers in late spring for several weeks before giving way to the hips. The rose hips ripen in the fall and will persist on the bush if animals and birds do not get them. While rose hips are known for their high vitamin C content, multiflora rose hips are not worth using because they are small and they do not have much flesh.

Pasture rose (*Rosa carolina*) is low growing, with pink flowers that bloom after multiflora rose. It too does not have very big rose hips. Another species of wild rose, *R. rugosa*, which is native to parts of Asia, has hips that are big enough to use; rugosa rose is commonly planted as an ornamental.

Where and When to Gather

Wild roses love sunny areas at the edge of woods, in flower beds, in disturbed soil, along fence lines, and in open fields. The flowers bloom in late spring and are easy to find because of their strong, sweet fragrance. The rose hips are not ready until late fall in the Southeast. They will be dark red and slightly soft when ripe.

How to Gather

Clip entire branches with the flowers attached. Be careful while handling the flowers because they are very delicate.

Gather the hips by using your hands to pull them off the stems, but be careful of the stems' prickly thorns. You can also clip a stem with several hips attached.

How to Eat

My favorite part of a rose is the petals. They have a sweet, heady scent. The best way to capture the fragrance is by infusing the petals in a liquid. Jellies, custards, and syrups are all excellent ways of using rose petal infusions. The nutritious hips can be used to make wine, tea, jelly, and vinegar. To use the hips, cut them in half, and scoop out the hairy seeds and discard.

How to Preserve

Keep the rose petals with damp paper towels on them in an airtight container in the refrigerator. Can the jellies or syrups made with the petals. To preserve the hips, first remove the hairy seeds, and then you can freeze them for up to three months for later use.

Future Harvests

Multiflora rose and pasture rose are invasive (as is rugosa rose, which grows more in the Northeast than the Southeast), so you can take as much as you want.

salsify

Tragopogon species

oyster plant

`EDIBLE` root, leaves, flowers

Salsify is a root vegetable that is cultivated by farmers for discerning chefs. The distinctive flavor of the root really is similar to oysters.

How to Identify

When salsify is in bloom, it looks a lot like dandelion. It has the recognizable yellow ray flowers and round, downy seed heads, and both plants exude a milky white sap when broken. The flowers open in the morning and close by midday. Salsify flowers have narrow, pointy bracts at their base. Once the plants go to seed, the bracts hang down. The seed heads themselves are much bigger than those of dandelion.

Salsify leaves are actually fairly different from dandelion leaves. They look like long blades of grass that first grow as narrow, untoothed rosette leaves up to 14 inches long. Shorter, alternate leaves clasp the

Salsify's yellow flowers in full bloom are a familiar sight.

1- to 5-foot-tall flower stalks. Salsify leaves look partially folded, or like they have a pleat down the middle. Salsify root looks like a beige carrot.

Where and When to Gather

Salsify likes full sunshine and disturbed soils. It grows in fields, along roadsides, and near the farms and gardens from which it escapes. Collect salsify leaves and crown (whole aboveground part of the plant) in early spring. When the flower stalks of this biennial plant have just begun to shoot up in April and are 1 foot or less high and still tender, cut the shoots off near the base. The unopened flower buds and top few inches of the flower stalks are ready to eat in early summer. Dig the root from fall through early spring.

How to Gather

Gather the leaves and crown by slicing off the top of the root with all the leaves still attached. Slice off the shoots near the base. Snap off the unopened flower buds a few inches down the flower stalks. Dig the first-year taproot that grows below the leaf rosettes with a shovel. The second-year taproot is too tough to eat.

How to Eat

You can eat the greens raw, but I prefer them cooked. Try them both ways and see what suits your taste. Lightly boiled or steamed, all they need is a little butter or extra virgin olive oil and salt. The root is my favorite part. It is excellent peeled, chopped, and added to soup or stew. It is also good in casseroles with cream sauces or cheese, and roasted. You can also batter and fry it.

How to Preserve

The root keeps well in a cellar or refrigerator if it is not allowed to dry out. The greens can be kept with a damp paper towel on top in an airtight container in the refrigerator up to a week.

Future Harvests

Salsify self-seeds well. There is no need to limit your harvest. But if you come across a field of salsify, just thin it out instead of harvesting everything.

saltwort

Batis maritima

EDIBLE leaves

Saltwort grows in salt marshes alongside glasswort. The flavor is saltier and sharper than glasswort, with a surprising juiciness.

How to Identify

Saltwort is a fleshy-leaved plant growing up to 3½ feet tall, but is usually less than 1 foot tall. It has trailing, arching, and erect stems that root at the nodes. The young stems are succulent, with alternate, cylindrical, yellowish green, fleshy leaves up to 1 inch long. Male and female flowers are borne on axillary spikes on separate plants, with the male flowers having overlapping scales and no stalks. The female flowers are short-stalked and produce fleshy fruit that grow in roundish clusters of two to eight.

The round leaves of saltwort are crunchy.

Where and When to Gather

Saltwort grows in salt marshes that are flooded from time to time. The best time to gather saltwort is in March and April.

How to Gather

Gather saltwort by pinching off a few cylindrical leaves from each plant.

How to Eat

Saltwort is salty and slightly watery, with a crunchy texture. It is best used raw. Use the cylindrical leaves in salads and with seafood.

How to Preserve

Keep saltwort in an airtight container in the refrigerator.

Future Harvests

Do not take all the leaves from this plant.

sassafras

Sassafras albidum

EDIBLE leaves, root

Sassafras is one of those plants that Southerners hear their grandparents or old-timers in the neighborhood talk about. All parts of the tree are aromatic, tasting and smelling like root beer.

How to Identify

Sassafras is a deciduous tree that grows up to 125 feet tall, and has reddish brown bark that is randomly split by cracks. The roots are very long and the root bark is very fragrant when scratched. The three different fragrant leaves are 3 to 5 inches long. One is oval, one looks like a mitten, and one has three lobes that looks like a goosefoot. The tiny, yellow, five-petaled flowers bloom in the spring. The ½-inch-long fruit is blue-black and egg-shaped, and appears in the summer.

Sassafras has three different shapes of leaves: oval, two-lobed, and three-lobed.

Where and When to Gather

Sassafras grows in old fields, open woodlands, bottomlands, and thickets. The best time to gather the leaves and roots is May through October.

How to Gather

Gather the leaves by clipping off a branch with leaves attached. The best way to gather the root is by digging it up. Sassafras has a long taproot, so it is difficult to dig up much, but you only need a small amount.

How to Eat

The leaves of sassafras can be dried and crushed into a powder called filé which is traditionally used to thicken gumbo. The green leaves can be used like bay leaf to flavor rice. From the root, you can make sassafras tea, which traditionally was used to cleanse the blood in the spring. Do not peel the bark off the root. Put the root in a pot of water and simmer until the water turns red. Sassafras tea can be used in a lot of ways: for syrups, sorbets, meat glazes, root beer, and sauce for braised shortribs.

How to Preserve

The root should be stored in an airtight container in the refrigerator. The leaves can be dried and ground for use in thickening liquids. Dry them by tying together branches with leaves attached and hang them upside down in a dry location. Once they are totally dry, you can crush the leaves by hand, or you can put them into a food processor and grind them for a finer grind.

Future Harvests

Where you find one sassafras tree, you will usually find more. If you do not, don't dig any up. Try to take parts of sassafras trees that are growing in the shade of another tree, because those will probably not reach full maturity. Sassafras trees take a while to grow, so harvest sparingly.

sea purslane

Sesuvium portulacastrum

EDIBLE young leaves

As you walk by a salt marsh, you may notice sea purslane growing alongside glasswort and saltwort. It has the same herbaceous saltiness as its companions, but is milder and the texture is more succulent.

How to Identify

Sea purslane is a creeping, mat-forming perennial herb. It has fleshy, succulent, spoon-shaped leaves that grow opposite each other and are up to 2 inches long on smooth stems that root at the nodes. The flowers are pink to light purple, with five "petals" that have a prominent tip at the end. Seeds are shiny.

Sea purslane looks similar to purslane that grows in gardens, but it grows in salt marshes.

Where and When to Gather

Sea purslane grows in salt marshes, sand flats, and the upper part of sandy beaches. The best time to gather the young leaves is March to early April.

How to Gather

Use scissors to snip off a section of the stem with leaves. Pick the leaves off the stem.

How to Eat

Sea purslane can be eaten raw or cooked. The flavor is salty like most plants that grow near the ocean. Use in salads, as a garnish, cook with potatoes and herbs, use in a tapenade instead of olives, or use with smoked fish.

How to Preserve

Keep the leaves of sea purslane with a damp paper towel in an airtight container in the refrigerator.

Future Harvests

Do not take all the leaves from sea purslane.

sea rocket

Cakile edentula
beach arugula, American searocket

EDIBLE leaves

Sea rocket is called beach arugula by many because it has a flavor similar to arugula, the cultivated green often called rocket.

How to Identify
Sea rocket is a low-growing, prostrate, multibranched annual growing up to 12 inches tall. Its fleshy, elliptical, alternate leaves are bluntly toothed and up to 2 inches long. The four-petaled flowers are pale purple to white.

Where and When to Gather
Sea rocket grows along beaches between the dunes and the high tide line. The best time to gather is in March. By April, sea rocket has started to flower and the flavor of the leaves is too strong.

This sea rocket is growing on a beach on the Atlantic Coast.

How to Gather

Gather the leaves of sea rocket by cutting.

How to Eat

The leaves of sea rocket are succulent. The texture and flavor are fantastic. The best way to use it is raw, but you could lightly steam it. Use the raw leaves in a salad with other greens or use as a garnish.

How to Preserve

Keep sea rocket with a damp paper towel on the leaves in an airtight container in the refrigerator.

Future Harvests

Once sea rocket starts to flower, stop harvesting. It will be back next year.

sheep sorrel

Rumex acetosella

EDIBLE leaves, stems

Sheep sorrel is a tasty little plant with succulent leaves that have a lemony, tart flavor.

How to Identify

Sheep sorrel gets its name from the shape of the leaves, which have a long face and two earlike lobes. This small perennial forms a basal rosette of spoon-shaped leaves. The leaves are succulent and grow up to 3 inches long. The flowering stalks, which grow up to 18 inches tall, are smooth and have a few small arrow-shaped leaves that form a fleur-de-lis shape. The stems are ridged, and tiny, reddish flowers grow along the upper portions of the stalk.

Sheep sorrel contains oxalic acid. In immense quantities, it can be toxic, so dairy is combined with sorrel in soups. In a normal human diet, it is not a concern. There are some poisonous plants with arrow-shaped leaves, but none are upright plants like sheep sorrel. Sheep sorrel contains lots of vitamin C.

Sheep sorrel basal leaves have a spoon shape.

Where and When to Gather

Sheep sorrel grows in fields, pastures, gardens, and disturbed soil. It loves acid soil. Where the ground is fertile, it will be fuller and more succulent. Sheep sorrel grows year-round, but its leaves and stems are best in spring and fall.

How to Gather

Gather sheep sorrel leaves, the best part of the plant, by cutting or pinching them off in the spring until the plant goes to seed and in the fall until it frosts.

How to Eat

Sheep sorrel can be eaten raw or cooked. Use raw sheep sorrel leaves in salads or as a garnish. Cooked sheep sorrel makes excellent sauces and soups. Sheep sorrel can also be used to make a tea. Just serve it with ice like lemonade.

How to Preserve

The leaves and stems should be stored with a damp paper towel in an airtight container in the refrigerator. You can make soup from the leaves and stems, and you can freeze or can them. You can also make a refreshing granita out of sheep sorrel lemonade.

Future Harvests

To ensure future harvesting, take just some of the leaves from a plant, and stop harvesting when it starts to flower.

shepherd's purse

Capsella bursa-pastoris

EDIBLE leaves, stalk

This is one of those wild plants you have walked past many times and never realized it was edible. The leaves and stalk have an appealing pepperiness.

Shepherd's purse has edible leaves.

How to Identify

Shepherd's purse is an annual that grows from a rosette of 2- to 4-inch, deeply lobed, toothed leaves. It has tiny, four-petaled white flowers that grow in loose racemes on flower stalks that vary from a few inches to 2 feet tall, depending on growing conditions. The flower stalks are either leafless or have a few leaves that are smaller than the rosette leaves and clasp the stalks at their bases.

The seed capsule is the most unique and easy-to-identify part of this plant. It is a flat, triangular- to heart-shaped pod up to 1/3 inch across that holds several reddish brown seeds. Supposedly the shape of the seedpod looked like the purse that shepherds used, giving the plant its common name.

Where and When to Gather

Shepherd's purse grows in full sun in disturbed soils. It is common in urban lots and gardens, as well as along rural roadsides. Gather the rosette leaves from March until the plants begin to flower. Gather the tender flower stalks when they are just starting to shoot up.

How to Gather

Handpick the leaves into a container and cut the flower stalk.

How to Eat

The small shepherd's purse leaves have a strong peppery flavor, so use them sparingly combined with other greens in a salad. I love to throw some in at the very end of a stir-fry. You can also bake them in a frittata or add some to an omelet. The flower stalk should be peeled before using.

How to Preserve

Store the greens and flower stalk with a damp paper towel on top in an airtight container in the refrigerator.

Future Harvests

There is no need to limit your harvest of this invasive plant.

The flat, triangular seedpods are key to identifying shepherd's purse.

shiso

Perilla frutescens
beefsteak plant

`EDIBLE` leaves, seeds

Shiso is the Japanese name for an herb that has a lemony earthiness. It is used often in Japan with sushi and beef. It grows wild all over the South in shady spots.

How to Identify

Shiso is a small annual that grows 12 to 36 inches tall and has opposite, coarsely toothed, 3- to 6-inch-long leaves. The underside of the leaves has a grayish purple color. The small flowers are white or purplish, producing very small seeds that reproduce prolifically. Many people grow shiso in their garden. There are green and reddish purple–leaved varieties of shiso. The green version is the true wild shiso; the reddish purple variety is a cultivated plant, which often escapes into the wild.

The leaves and seeds of shiso are edible.

Where and When to Gather

Shiso grows along trails, roads, at the edge of woods, and in disturbed soil in mostly shady areas. It will start to come up in late June when summer starts to get hot.

How to Gather

Gather shiso by cutting the stem. Do not just pull leaves off the plant.

How to Eat

Shiso can be used raw or cooked. The flavor is complex, earthy, and slightly lemony. The green variety is much more fragrant than the cultivated variety. Shiso works especially well with fish and meat. If you are using it raw, it is excellent with mint in marinades and salads. Use the seeds as a spice or infuse them into salt.

How to Preserve

Store the leaves with a damp paper towel in an airtight container in the refrigerator.

Future Harvests

Shiso can be invasive in some areas. Even so, always leave some behind. When gathering shiso, be sure to cut at the stem. This ensures that the plant will produce new branches with leaves so it will keep growing all summer.

Solomon's seal

Polygonatum biflorum

EDIBLE rhizomes, young shoots

Walking along a hiking trail, you may notice this beautiful arching plant, Solomon's seal. The young shoots of this plant have a strong, tasty asparagus flavor.

The flowers of Solomon's seal hang in pairs from along the stem rather than from the tip of the plant in clusters like they do on false Solomon's seal.

How to identify

Solomon's seal is a woodland perennial that grows 1 to 4 feet tall in a single, arching stem that rises from knotty, white rhizomes. The alternate, elliptical leaves grow in two rows 2 to 6 inches long and have parallel veins. The flowers are drooping, bell-like, and whitish green with six short lobes. The ¼-inch spherical fruit, which develops in August, is dark bluish black.

Where and When to Gather

Solomon's seal grows in rich, moist wooded areas. Gather the rhizomes in early April and the young shoots in early May.

How to Gather

Dig up the rhizomes with a shovel and break off the shoots at the most tender section of the stem. When harvesting the shoots, be sure to gather before the leaves unfurl, when the plant will turn acrid.

How to Eat

The rhizomes are best eaten raw. You can use them like burdock in a soup, but the Solomon's seal rhizomes are stronger than burdock. The shoots taste like asparagus, but stronger. Use the shoots in any way you would asparagus. I love to simply grill the shoots with sea salt, lemon, and olive oil.

How to Preserve

Keep the rhizomes and shoots with a damp paper towel on top in an airtight container in the refrigerator.

Future Harvests

Only collect a little at a time. Solomon's seal takes a long time to grow and is susceptible to overharvest.

Warning

The dark black berries of Solomon's seal may look enticing, but they are not edible.

sow thistle

Sonchus oleraceus

EDIBLE flower stalk, florets, young leaves

Sow thistle drives farmers crazy by coming up in their pastures and spreading. Animals do not eat sow thistle, but with a little bit of work, they are delicious for us. The flower stalk is like celery in texture and flavor, the tender young leaves are tasty greens, and the florets of sow thistle have a wonderful bittersweet flavor.

How to Identify

Sow thistle gets its name from pigs, which love to devour the plant. It is a perennial that looks like dandelion or wild lettuce. It comes up in disturbed soil, fields, and vacant lots. It grows up to 8 feet tall, with toothed, prickly-edged leaves that are 1 to 2 inches across. The yellow flowers look like dandelion blossoms and grow in branched clusters.

There are several different species of sow thistle. Field sow thistle (*Sonchus arvensis*) has thinner stalks with large dandelionlike flowers and leaves that are not

This sow thistle is getting ready to bloom.

lobed. Prickly sow thistle (*S. asper*) leaves are not as deeply lobed and have big prickles on the leaf edge.

Where and When to Gather
Sow thistle grows any place the soil has been disturbed. The leaves of sow thistle should be gathered in March and April while they are still young and tender. Once the plant sends up a stalk, the leaves become tough and bitter. The stalk can be gathered at any time until the plant starts to flower. Gather the florets any time before they open up.

How to Gather
Harvest the flower stalk, young leaves, and florets of sow thistle by cutting or breaking them off.

How to Eat
The stalks of sow thistle can be cooked or eaten raw. I feel that the edible stalk of the plant is one of the most underutilized parts, and I love the crunchy texture. Before eating, peel off the tough, bitter outer layer of the stalk. The texture of the stem is like celery. Use it in salads, pickled, or with the young leaves in a salad. The leaves also can be cooked. The florets are delicious sautéed or stir-fried.

How to Preserve
You can pickle the stalks or candy the florets.

Future Harvests
Do not worry about limiting your harvest. Sow thistle self-seeds readily.

spicebush

Lindera benzoin

EDIBLE leaves, fruit, twigs

Spicebush provides some of my favorite seasonings: it has peppery berries and aromatic leaves that impart a citrus and floral fragrance.

How to Identify

Spicebush is a medium-size deciduous 5- to 15-foot-tall shrub that grows in the forest understory. There are both male and female plants, although you may only notice the difference in late summer and early fall when the female shrubs have red, oval berries about ⅓ inch long, each with a single relatively large seed inside. You may find already full-size berries earlier in the summer, but they will be green. The leaves are more or less oval in shape, 2 to 6 inches long, with smooth margins and pointed tips. They grow alternately on the branches with the pointed end of the leaf being ever so slightly lopsided. Spicebush leaves are

Spicebush produces aromatic red berries.

tender and delicate, even when large. To confirm your identification, crush one of the leaves to release its strong fragrance, with both citrus and floral notes.

The bark of both the male and female plants is gray-brown and speckled with lenticels, which are small, corky spots on the bark of shrubs and small trees. Winter flower buds on the branches are easy to identify with their orblike shapes, each wrapped in two to three scales. Like the leaves and berries, the twigs and buds also have spicebush's intense fragrance.

Where and When to Gather

Spicebush grows in woodlands where the soil is rich and moist, often along streams. The twigs may be used throughout the year. Gather the fresh leaves throughout the summer. You can use the fresh leaves and twigs of both male and female spicebush shrubs. The ripe berries are in season from late summer through early fall.

How to Gather

If you are harvesting the twigs, snip just a few inches off each branch with a knife or pruners to make clean cuts. Gather the fresh leaves by taking just a few leaves. Do not strip all the leaves off a branch, which inhibits the growth of the plant. Pinch the ripe berries off into containers.

How to Eat

The fresh leaves make a really good iced tea. They don't dry well, and brewing the tea with boiling or hot water over the leaves brings out an unpleasant bitter edge. A cold-water infusion captures the aroma and tastes best. Simply crush a few fresh leaves in your hand and place in a glass jar along with cold or room-temperature water. Cover the jar and leave it in the sun for two to six hours. Strain out the leaves and chill.

Spicebush twigs also make a good tea. Snap these into pieces approximately 1 inch long or smaller. Use 2 tablespoons of twigs to 1 cup of water. Pour a cup of boiling water over the twigs. Cover the container and let steep for ten to fifteen minutes. Strain out the twigs and sweeten to taste with honey. Do not boil or simmer the twigs; it makes this beverage more bitter than aromatic.

My favorite part of the spicebush plant is the berries. These are found only on the female shrubs and can be used fresh or dried. Some people say that the berries taste like allspice. I think the dried berries have a flavor closer to black pepper, while the leaves have a citrusy scent.

Some Native American tribes separate the pulp and skin of the berries from the seed and dry them as two different spices. The seed has a hotter, more peppery taste than the sweeter skin and pulp. But that is a labor-intensive process, and they taste so good together that I rarely bother.

Spicebush berries work equally well in sweet and savory recipes. I use them in marinades, rubs, and dipping sauces for vegetables, meat, and poultry, but I also flavor desserts with them.

To use fresh spicebush berries, grind them in a food processor. Grind dried spicebush berries in an electric or manual coffee or spice grinder.

How to Preserve
Spicebush berries have a high fatty oil content that can turn rancid. To avoid this, store them in the freezer or refrigerator. Store them whole, and grind as needed. Spicebush leaves lose a lot of their flavor when they are dried, but the twigs can be dried successfully. Store them in paper or cloth in a dry place with good air circulation for one to two weeks.

Future Harvests
Do not strip a whole spicebush of all the different edible parts. Take a little bit from here and a little from there to ensure a healthy plant.

spiderwort

Tradescantia virginiana

spider lily

`EDIBLE` flowers, leaves, stems, seeds

A plant that is native to the eastern United States, spiderwort grows like a weed in urban spaces. Its leaves, stems, flowers, and seeds can all be eaten. One of the few plants that grow during the heat of the summer, it produces leaves that have a mild green bean flavor, perfect for salads. The purple flowers have a crunchy texture and a mild flavor.

Spiderwort is a robust plant with beautiful violet-blue to purple flowers.

How to Identify

Spiderwort is an herbaceous perennial that grows up to 3 feet tall and has long, narrow leaves. Its stunning terminal flowers have three round, blue-violet petals and golden stamens and are up to 1½ inches across. Spiderwort is a close relative of Asiatic dayflower (*Commelina communis*), which is also edible.

Where and When to Gather

Spiderwort comes up in gardens, open woods, and disturbed areas. The young leaves appear in early spring and the flowers start blooming in late spring to early summer.

How to Gather

The young leaves, stems, flowers, and seeds can be eaten raw or cooked. Clip or pinch off the young leaves and flowers. To use the seeds, open the flower in the summer to find them.

How to Eat

The purple flowers are gorgeous as a garnish or candied. The leaves and stems have a mild green-bean flavor that makes a tasty contribution to a salad. The seeds, which taste like green peas, are excellent added at the last minute to rice dishes and stir-fries.

How to Preserve

I like to pickle the stems and young leaves.

Future Harvests

Spiderwort is prolific. Even though it is an annual, there is no need to limit your harvest.

stinging nettle

Urtica dioica

EDIBLE leaves, stem

Stinging nettle is one of the most popular wild edibles used by restaurants. The leaves and stems are highly nutritious and have a deeply herbal flavor. They can be added to dishes, served as a nutritious side dish or greens, or made into tea. When cooked or dried, the sting magically disappears.

How to Identify

Stinging nettle is an herbaceous perennial that comes up in fields, open woods, and thickets in rich soil. It has a ribbed, hollow stem that grows 2 to 7 feet tall, with oval, dark green, opposite leaves that are rough, pointed, and coarsely toothed. Tiny stinging hairs cover the stem and leaves, which will produce an intense, stinging pain if you just brush up against them lightly

Stinging nettle may look harmless but it really does sting.

when walking by. The sting feels like a jellyfish sting. The male and female flowers grow on different plants. The flower clusters are tiny, and hang in paired strands from the leaf axils.

Wood nettle (*Laportea canadensis*) looks very similar, but has alternate, oval leaves. It has fewer stinging hairs, but it will still sting you. It tastes just like stinging nettle.

Where and When to gather

Stinging nettle grows in fields, open woodlands, and shady areas. It starts to appear in late spring and grows until the first frost. Harvest leaves and stems before flowering.

How to Gather

Gather stinging nettle at any time up until it starts to bloom. Always wear gloves and cut above where leaves branch out when collecting stinging nettle. That way the plant will keep growing.

How to Eat

Wear gloves while preparing fresh stinging nettle. The leaves and stem can be eaten cooked. Stinging nettle is a versatile ingredient, and is good in soups, sauces, pestos, quiches, as a side dish, and made into a tea.

How to Preserve

Dry the leaves for tea. Nettle tea is delicious and good for you. It is a good tonic when feeling run down.

Future Harvests

Even though stinging nettle is a hardy perennial, harvest a limited amount from an established group of plants.

sumac

Rhus species

EDIBLE fruit, shoots

Sumac—when you hear that word, you may automatically think of poison sumac. But sumac looks nothing like poison sumac, and its fruit is one of my favorite summer wild edibles for its sharp, sour, and tart flavor.

How to Identify

There are several edible sumacs in our region. Smooth sumac (*Rhus glabra*), common in the Southeast, grows 3 to 10 feet tall, and has alternate, pointed, sharply toothed leaves 2 to 2¾ inches long. Male and female flowers grow on separate plants in cone-shaped clusters. The tiny green flower buds become upright, open clusters of rust-colored blooms and produce tiny fruits that start out white, slowly turn red, and have tiny hairs covering them. The ripe red berries are also covered in a white bloom of ascorbic acid. The leaves typically turn a brilliant scarlet in the fall.

In the northern portions of our region, staghorn sumac (*Rhus typhina*) is familiar. It is almost identical to smooth sumac, but can grow up to 25 feet, and the fruit clusters are tighter and look like spearheads. Staghorn sumac can be used just like smooth sumac.

Where and When to Gather

Smooth sumac grows in old fields, disturbed soil, at the edge of woods, and along roads. The shoots of first-year plants, which are small and not woody, should be gathered from April to May. The fruits usually develop the white bloom starting in July. Rain often washes away the ascorbic acid, so be sure to watch the fruit clusters for the right time to harvest.

How to Gather

Break off the shoots of smooth sumac with your hands. Clip with shears or break off the red fruit clusters. Bring along a bucket or pail to hold the harvest, because the ascorbic acid fruit coating will rub off inside plastic bags.

How to Eat

To use sumac as an infusion, fill a bowl with clean, cold water. Submerge the fruit and rub the ascorbic acid and red color into the water. Strain any debris from the liquid. With the tart, sour, pink liquid, you can make several items. You can easily make a sumac-ade, and the flavor of smooth sumac works really well in cocktails. It is also excellent made into a sauce for grilled game. You can dry the fruits with the ascorbic acid on them and then

The white bloom coating sumac's red berries is pure ascorbic acid, which is vitamin C.

grind them into a powder. Sumac is a component of za'atar, a Middle Eastern spice blend with mild, tart, lemony flavor.

The shoots need to have their thin outer skin peeled before eating. The texture of the shoots is crunchy with a surprisingly sweet flavor that is nothing like the tart, sour berries. The peeled shoots make a great snack.

How to Preserve

Sumac lasts well at room temperature. But if you are storing it for some time, refrigerate it in an airtight container. To dry it, harvest the fruit clusters with the coating of ascorbic acid still present and hang in a dry, well-ventilated area until completely dry. Then carefully pull off the berries into

a bowl and discard any debris like small branches. Place the dried berries into a coffee grinder or spice grinder, grind until smooth, and store in an airtight container.

Future Harvests

Sumac is common, but take only a few fruit clusters from a plant.

Warning

Poison sumac (*Toxicodendron vernix*, formerly *Rhus vernix*) grows in boggy, swampy areas and has white berries that droop. The plant resembles smooth sumac, but smooth sumac does not grow in those areas and the ripe red fruit clusters do not droop.

violet

Viola species

leaves, flowers

Violets, with their delicate purple, yellow, or white blossoms, are among my favorite springtime plants. The flowers are gorgeous candied, and the leaves have a slight peppery flavor and a chewy texture.

How to Identify

Violets are perennials growing up to 8 inches tall with a basal rosette of heart-shaped leaves 2 to 4 inches long and wide. The blue or white flowers have five petals in a butterfly shape. Blue is the most common color of violet flowers. The flowers you see are not the true flower, however: the true flower is a small, brown flower growing at ground level, which makes tiny, round, purplish seeds. Violet flowers are sterile, and the plants spread

Violets have edible flowers and leaves.

by underground rhizomes. That is why you find them in patches.

Where and When to Gather
Violets grow in yards and disturbed soil. They start to bloom in mid-spring and grow until the fall. Gather the flowers and leaves at any time. The leaves are best while they are still young. Once the heat of summer hits them, they get stringy.

How to Gather
Use your hand to pinch off the flowers and place them into a container by your feet. The leaves should be cut with shears.

How to Eat
Violet flowers are among my favorite wild salad ingredients. They do not taste like much, but look gorgeous as a garnish on just about anything. They also work beautifully when candied in sugar, which is a great way to preserve them. The flowers can also be infused into syrups. The chewy leaves are mucilaginous, so if you do cook them, use them as a thickener in soups and stews.

How to Preserve
Candy the flowers or infuse them in a simple syrup. The leaves can be dried to use in soups and stews to thicken them.

Future Harvests
Gathering the blue or white flowers will not harm the plant. Do not take all the leaves from a plant.

Warning
There are a few poisonous plants that have flowers similar to violet flowers. Dwarf larkspur (*Delphinium tricorne*) has a spur sticking out of the back of its violet-hued, five-petaled flower. Southern blue monkshood (*Aconitum uncinatum*) has large, helmetlike flowers. Both plants are very poisonous.

Virginia pine

Pinus virginiana

EDIBLE green pine needles, young tips, buds, pollen

There is nothing more representative of nature in the South than the pine tree. There are several species of pine in the Southeast, and you see them wherever you go. The needles of Virginia pine have a strong citrus and pine fragrance, are nutritious, and make a good tea.

How to Identify

Several different types of pine trees grow in the Southeast. Loblolly pine (*Pinus taeda*) and shortleaf pine (*P. echinata*) are common, and you will occasionally come across longleaf pine (*P. palustris*). My favorite, though, is Virginia pine (*P. virginiana*), which is a 40- to 70-foot-tall scrubby-looking tree with pairs of twisted needles 2 to 3 inches long. The pine needles of this species are extremely fragrant. They smell very piney, and citrusy like grapefruit. Pine needles contain up to five times the amount of vitamin C found in a lemon. They make a delicious tea that is effective for treating coughs and colds.

Virginia pine has been grown as a Christmas tree.

Virginia pine has pairs of long needles.

The dormant buds of Virginia pine start growing in early spring, and elongate into what are called candles. As they start to elongate, male cones are produced. Male and female cones are produced on the same tree. The male cones produce pollen, which triggers a strong allergic reaction in many people. The buds of pine, before they start to elongate, are used in northern Italy to make a syrup called muglio, which is highly prized for its unique woodsy, piney, complex flavor. Virginia pine and other pine species in the Southeast do not produce pine nuts, like other species in the western states such as the pinyon pine and gray pine.

Where and When to Gather

While pine trees do grow in moist and dry soil in every type of terrain, they grow best in acidic soil. They stay evergreen all year, but the flavor and fragrance of the needles are best in the fall, winter, and spring.

How to Gather

The green pine needles, pollen, and buds can be eaten. Gather green pine needles by clipping a few small branches. If gathering pine buds, gather just a few from several trees. To gather pine pollen, hold a small container beneath the buds in springtime and shake the branch.

How to Eat

Use the green pine needles to make tea, smoke meats, infuse into liquids like milk or vodka, or as a roasting bed. (To make pine needle tea, see Infusing Liquids, page 19.) The needles can also be finely chopped and used like rosemary. You can make syrup with the young pine buds and you can also pickle them. Even though the pollen does not taste like much, it turns pasta and gnocchi dough a beautiful, golden yellow. Besides lending color to pastas, it is also high in testosterone.

How to Preserve

The young pine buds are tasty when candied or pickled. You can make pine needle tea and freeze it.

Future Harvests

Pine needles lose their flavor during the summer time, so that's a good time to stop harvesting and give the tree a rest. Cut just a few branches when gathering pine needles to ensure that the tree keeps growing.

Warning

Pine needles contain phytoestrogens, and cattle consuming pine needles, specifically from ponderosa pine (*Pinus ponderosa*), have been documented to have miscarriages. Pregnant women are therefore advised not to consume pine in any form.

wapato

Sagittaria latifolia

arrowhead, katniss

EDIBLE tubers, young leaves, leafstalks, immature flower stalks

Wapato grows in or at the edges of water. So you may have to get wet and muddy to enjoy this wild plant's edible parts. The tubers are delicious: they taste like potato mixed with a sweet corn flavor. The young leaves and stalks, when cooked, have a pleasant herbal flavor.

How to Identify

Wapato is found in wetlands or shallow ponds. The leaves typically have an arrow shape—one large point at the tip and two narrower points at the stem end—from which they get one of their common names, arrowhead. But there is one southern species, *Sagittaria rigida*, that does not form those two back lobes but instead is lance-shaped, linear, or oval.

Two other aquatic species that have similarly shaped leaves and frequently grow alongside wapato are pickerelweed (see page 184) and arrow arum (*Peltandra*

Wapato has distinctive arrowhead-shaped leaves.

virginica). Pickerelweed's hind lobes are rounded rather than pointed. Arrow arum's veins branch off a central vein, whereas wapato veins fan out from the base of the leaf.

Wapato's white, three-petaled flowers have a green knob at the center. In the fall, long after the petals have fallen away, these central knobs turn brown and eventually fall apart to disseminate winged seeds. Each plant produces several tubers, and each tuber is solo on the end of an unbranched rhizome. They vary in size from a marble to a small egg, and the tuber color varies from brown to purple to off-white. Each tuber has one curved shoot, and usually a ring or two with a membranous wrapping. In the spring, that single sickle-shaped shoot grows toward the top of the mud, where it forms a knob that then sends forth the aerial parts of the plant.

Where and When to Gather

Wapato grows in mud in shallow, fresh water. The tubers can be harvested from late summer through early spring. Gather the leaves and leafstalks when the leaves are still furled. Harvest the flower stalks when they begin to shoot up but before the flowers open.

How to Gather

I recommend wearing tall rubber boots and using a shovel or potato rake to gather the tubers. Some people also use their feet to dislodge the tubers from the mud. Harvest wapato by working the mud back and forth with your tool of choice, dislodging the top few inches of muck. Soon, you'll get to the top of the tuber layer. Keep moving the muck, and eventually you'll dislodge tubers that will float to the surface. I usually go in with a shovel and start by moving aside the top few inches of mud that don't harbor any tasty tubers. Some of the wapato tubers may be rotten. If they smell rotten, they are. Skip those. Cut off the leaves and flower stalks with a pocketknife or scissors.

How to Eat

Wash the tubers, then slice off and discard both the shoot end and the opposite end where the tuber was attached to the rhizome. Peel the tubers with a vegetable peeler. The skin of the tubers is bitter and imparts the bitterness when cooked. Cook wapato tubers any way you prepare potatoes. The young leaves, leafstalks, and immature flower stalks are quite good once cooked. Raw, they have a citrus peel flavor, and cooking removes most of that flavor.

How to Preserve

Boil wapato tubers and mash them, then dry and grind the mash to make a "flour." Use the wapato flour to make gnocchi. You can also make vodka with the tubers, using a sweet potato or potato vodka recipe. The tubers can be sliced and pickled.

Future Harvests

There is no need to limit your harvest of this prolific plant.

watercress

Nasturtium officinale

`EDIBLE` leaves

Watercress is one of the most sought-after wild edibles. The leaves and leafstalks have a pleasing crunchiness. The pepperiness of its leaves pairs well with citrus, seafood, and beef.

How to Identify

Watercress is a low-growing plant in the mustard family that is usually under 12 inches tall. It form mats in shallow, cool, moving, fresh spring water. The 1½- to 6-inch-long leaves are deeply lobed, with the rounded lobes lined up in pairs along the midrib and a single large lobe at the end. Watercress flowers, which are tiny and white, have four petals in a cross shape and grow in clusters. Watercress seed capsules are very narrow and about ¾ inch long.

Where and When to Gather

Like all plants growing in water, watercress is only as clean as the water in which it is growing. That is one reason why wild watercress is so hard to find. Often, the

In the Southeast, watercress appears in November.

water will be polluted with runoff from farm animals or is full of parasites that can make you extremely sick. Have the water tested before harvesting. Some people say that you can boil watercress to remove any impurities, but I prefer watercress raw so I can enjoy the crunchy texture.

Look for watercress in ditches, shallow ponds, and spring-fed streams. Watercress can be harvested in the Southeast from November until April when it starts to bloom. After that, the flavor is too strong.

How to Gather

I harvest watercress by cutting it with scissors. You can also snap off the leafstalks by hand.

How to Eat

Watercress has a tangy horseradish flavor. Each patch of watercress has a slightly different flavor. Some will be well balanced, while others will be extremely peppery. You can eat watercress raw or cooked. Watercress is fantastic in salads with citrus. It is also really good with seafood and beef. If you do cook watercress, add it at the very end in a stir-fry. Traditionally in France, watercress is used to make a cream-based soup.

How to Preserve

You can add the leaves to kimchi, or blanch and freeze them to make soup later.

Future Harvests

Never harvest watercress by pulling the whole plant up. By cutting leaves, you are ensuring that the plant will continue to regrow.

Warning

Water hemlock (*Cicuta maculata*), a deadly poisonous plant, sometimes grows together with watercress. Water hemlock leaves are more pointed and more yellow-green than those of watercress, and the plants are much taller (up to 3 to 5 feet when mature). Also, water hemlock has leaf veins that end *between* the pointed teeth rather than at the points.

white clover

Trifolium repens

EDIBLE flower heads

White clover is less conspicuous than red clover, but the white pom-pom blooms of white clover are sweeter.

How to Identify

White clover leaflets grow in a grouping of three, and usually have a whitish mark. The leaves are squat and roundish, and grow on 1- to 3-inch leafstalks. The plants can get to be slightly more than 1 foot high, but are frequently shorter. The white flowers are made up of many individual florets. They are usually only ½ inch across, but may get bigger if growing in rich, moist soil.

Where and When to Gather

Look for white clover in sunny fields and lawns. Gather white clover any time it is in bloom, from April to October.

The blooms of white clover are like tiny pom-poms.

How to Gather

Pinch off the pom-pomlike flower heads with your hands.

How to Eat

Use white clover blossoms in the ways you use the blossoms of red clover (see page 206). The flowers are good fresh or fully dried. They make an excellent tea. The flowers have a small, tough central core and base to which the tiny florets are attached. This isn't a problem if you are making tea, but for other uses, I recommend that you strip the tender florets off the tough core and base.

How to Preserve

Place whole white clover flowers between two fine-mesh screens, and spread them out in a single layer. Leave in a dry place away from direct light or heat until the leaves are easy to crumble and the flowers are completely dry.

Future Harvests

There is no need to limit your harvest.

wild carrot

Daucus carota
Queen Anne's lace

EDIBLE roots, young leaves, seeds

Like other wild plants that have cultivated counterparts, wild carrot tastes a lot stronger than conventional store-bought carrots. Besides using the root, the seeds taste similar to coriander but with an intense carrot flavor.

How to Identify

Wild carrot leaves look like those of domesticated carrot. They are the same species, and the biggest difference is that wild carrot's taproot is off-white rather than orange. Look for finely divided, feathery leaves that smell like carrots when crushed. It is important to look at

These white, lacy flowers of wild carrot are in full bloom.

the leafstalks. Wild carrot's leafstalks are hairy. None of its poisonous look-alikes have hairy leafstalks.

Wild carrot is a biennial, and in its first year of growth, the plant produces only a rosette of lacy leaves. The following year, it sends up flower stalks. The flowers are flat, lacy umbels of tiny white florets. There may or may not be a single purple floret in the center of the umbel, but if there is, that is one of the confirming identification characteristics of wild carrot. There are long, curved, three-forked bracts under the flower umbels. The bract under the umbels of poison hemlock, by contrast, looks like a tiny leaf and is not forked.

The flowers bear seeds that look and smell a little like a mix of caraway and fennel seeds. They are covered with hairs. What was the flat flower umbel folds up around the seeds into a cup like a bird's nest, which enables you to locate wild carrot even in winter. Poison hemlock does not form a bird's nest cup, nor do its seeds have hairs.

Where and When to Gather

Look for wild carrot in sunny fields, in disturbed soils, city lots, and along roadsides. You will also commonly find it in gardens and parks. Gather the leaves from spring through fall. The roots are ready to harvest from fall through early spring. The seeds are ready from late summer through early fall, but they have the best flavor when they are either green or newly turned brown.

How to Gather

Break off the leafstalks by hand. Dig the roots with a shovel or trowel, and only bother digging the roots of first-year plants that have just a leaf rosette and no flower stalks. Collect the seed heads by snapping off their stalks.

How to Eat

Wild carrot roots taste like carrots but can be woodier. Use them for their flavor instead of on their own. You can grate them for use in a slaw or finely chop the roots to use as a base seasoning in soups and stews. Sometimes the core of a wild carrot root is too tough to eat, but it can be easily removed. Simply cut the root in half lengthwise and strip out the woody core. Use the leaves sparingly as a dill-like herb. Use the seeds like fennel or dill seeds. I also like to use the seeds in rye bread in place of caraway seeds.

How to Preserve

Dried wild carrot seeds will keep for a year in an airtight jar.

Future Harvests

Wild carrot is considered invasive in many parts of the South. There is no need to limit your harvest.

Warning

Wild carrot seeds have been used as a sort of herbal morning-after pill. Pregnant women or women trying to become pregnant should not eat the seeds.

wild ginger

Asarum canadense

EDIBLE leaves, stems, rhizomes

The rhizomes of wild ginger do not look like the knobby roots of ginger you will find at a market or store. They are long and stringy with the familiar ginger flavor, but with a floral, pepperiness too.

How to Identify

Wild ginger is an herbaceous perennial that grows as a ground cover between 6 to 12 inches tall. Its heart-shaped leaves are 3 to 6 inches across, grow in pairs, and are velvety, with smooth edges. Underneath the leaves at ground level, you will find its distinctive purplish brown, three-pointed, bell-shaped, 1-inch flowers. These spring wildflowers are under the leaves because the plants are pollinated by ants. The plants spread by horizontal rhizomes.

Where and When to Gather

Wild ginger grows in partial to full shade. It loves moist woodlands. You can collect wild ginger from spring through fall.

Wild ginger looks nothing like the cultivated variety.

How to Gather

Do not harvest wild ginger unless you find a substantial patch, and when you do, only take a small percentage of the leaves. Use a shovel to dig up the rhizomes. When you dig them up, some of the rhizomes will invariably break off. Replant them, and they will regrow, forming new plants.

How to Eat

Wild ginger can be used in sweet or savory dishes. You can make ice cream and sorbet from the root. Ginger root also works really well mashed up with a mortar and pestle and added to a lime vinaigrette. It can be used in many Asian dishes. Make a wild ginger simple syrup from the leaves, stem, or root, and use it in your next cocktail.

How to Preserve

I love to use the stem and leaves to infuse grain alcohol or vodka for a liqueur.

You can candy or pickle the rhizomes, stems, and leaves.

Future Harvests

Wild ginger is a slow-growing native plant and in some places is endangered by foragers who overharvest by indiscriminately pulling it up by the roots. Collect only a fraction of what you find. If you do collect the roots, gather only a few here and there.

Warning

Wild ginger can contain aristolochic acid, which in large quantities can cause serious kidney problems. Treat it as a seasoning, not a vegetable. If you already have kidney problems, I recommend not using it.

wild grape

Vitis species

`EDIBLE` fruit, leaves

Wild grape species grow all over the Southeast and come in different shapes and sizes. You can enjoy wild grapes in the same ways you enjoy cultivated varieties.

How to Identify

Wild grapes are woody vines with maple-like leaves that can grow as big as 8 inches across. The leaves have three lobes and the undersides are usually feltlike. The vines have forked tendrils for latching onto other plants and structures to climb toward more sunlight. The clusters of aromatic, small, greenish flowers have five petals. These become the grapes. Most wild grapes are deep purple when ripe. Each grape has several seeds.

The two grapes most widespread in the Southeast are muscadine and winter or frost grapes. You will also find summer grapes. These three edible wild grapes

Muscadine, a type of wild grape in the South, becomes entangled with other plants as it grows.

Winter or frost grapes hang in clusters of tiny fruit.

grow in overgrown fields, on trees, and at the edge of woods. They are among those from which cultivated grapes came.

Muscadine (*Vitis rotundifolia*) grows like other wild grapes, but with smaller leaves and bigger fruit. The fruit of wild muscadine is smaller and has a tougher skin than cultivated counterparts. Winter grape (*V. vulpina*) has huge leaves and clusters of small red grapes. Locally they are sometimes called fox grapes. Summer grape (*V. aestivalis*) has leaves that are different from other wild grapes—deeply lobed, with three to five lobes—and it produces small fruit that turns dark purple or black when ripe.

Where and When to Gather

Wild grapes grow in full to partial sun where they can climb on something, be it a tree or a fence. They frequently grow in and on thickets, by streams and river-banks, and near the shore. Collect grape leaves when they are big enough to stuff but the veins haven't become too tough, usually in late spring to early summer. The fruit is ripe from late summer into fall. Frost grapes turn sweet after a frost.

How to Gather

The leaves and the whole fruit clusters are easy to harvest by snapping them off by hand.

How to Eat

Dolmas, a Greek dish of stuffed grape leaves, is popular. I love to make dolmas stuffed with Carolina Gold rice seasoned with dried sumac. Why go to the store to buy grape leaves out of a can when they grow wild all around us?

To use the fruit to make wine and jelly, you first need to extract the juice. Wild grapes are not as sweet as cultivated ones, and many of them are so high in tartrate that the freshly extracted juice can give your skin a burning sensation. The way to get tartrate-free wild grape juice is to let the juice sit for a day or two, and then pour it off, leaving behind the tartrate substance that has settled at the bottom of the container.

The tender vine tendrils make a tasty raw snack. You can also use the vines to smoke meats. The next time you smoke quail or salmon, throw some green wild grape vines in the smoker.

How to Preserve

Grape leaves can be blanched and frozen. Once free of tartaric acid, the juice can be canned or frozen. Wild grape jelly and wine are delicious traditional ways to preserve the harvest.

Future Harvests

There is no need to limit your harvest.

wild lettuce

Lactuca species

leaves

Wild lettuce has a pleasant bitter lettuce flavor that I cannot get enough of. The flavor and texture of the leaves are reminiscent of dandelion and romaine lettuce. These flavors combine to make it an excellent green salad.

How to Identify

There are several different types of wild lettuce. The most common, wild lettuce (*Lactuca canadensis*), grows in a rosette with widely variable leaves. Some are deeply lobed, while others are barely toothed. It also has small, light hairs on the underside of the midrib. All types of wild lettuce excrete a milky sap when cut. This sap is where the lettuce's bitterness comes from. In fact, if you let the white sap dry and turn brown, it gets even more bitter.

Wild lettuce is delicious.

Wild lettuce produces tall stalks that can reach over 6 feet tall with small, yellow, dandelionlike flowers branching out from the top of the stem. Dandelion looks similar, but is hairless. Prickly lettuce (*L. scariola*) has prickles on the edges of the leaves, and hairy lettuce (*L. hirsuta*) has hairs on the leaves.

Where and When to Gather

Wild lettuce grows in disturbed soil, fields, forests, and gardens. It starts appearing in the fall and slowly grows during the winter, before it really gets going in the spring. The best time to gather wild lettuce is in late winter and early spring.

How to Gather

Cut or break off the leaves individually at any time up until the plant starts to send up a flower stalk. When the plant starts to flower and bolt, the leaves get too bitter.

How to Eat

Wild lettuce is best eaten raw in salads, either a leafy or a composed vegetable salad.

How to Preserve

Wild lettuce is best used fresh. To preserve the freshness, keep a damp paper towel on the leaves in an airtight container in the refrigerator. Wild lettuce will last for about a week this way.

Future Harvests

Wild lettuce self-seeds. But leave some behind when you are picking, so the plant can regrow.

wild onion

Allium canadense
meadow garlic, wild garlic

EDIBLE leaves, bulbs, flowers, seeds

Wild onion is a perennial that comes up in fields as well as in yards. It is not as common as field garlic, but just as flavorful. The distinguishing flat leaves have a strong onion flavor.

How to Identify

Wild onion has flat leaves, and grows from underground bulbs up to 14 inches tall. The bulbs look like tiny onions that grow together, and propagate by splitting off from each other. Wild onion blooms in late spring with pink to white flowers in pom-pom clusters. The blooms appear earlier than field garlic flowers. The flowers are replaced by bulbets that will grow threadlike green tendrils. These will eventually fall to the ground and grow into new plants.

Wild onion has an edible bulb and leaves that smell and taste just like a cultivated onion.

Where and When to Gather

Wild onions grow in fields, disturbed soil, lawns, and open woods. It starts coming up in the fall and can be harvested during the winter and spring. Be extremely careful about harvesting alliums from vacant lots in a city, because they absorb heavy metals from the soil.

How to Gather

You can gather wild onion anytime it is growing. The whole plant from the roots to the top can be eaten. Harvest by digging up the whole plant or snipping the green tops off.

How to Eat

Wild onions are more pungent than cultivated onions. Use the green tops like chives. The bulbs with roots attached are excellent fried in a tempura batter. Chop up the whole plant to use in broths and soups. Use wild onions in any way you would store-bought onions.

How to Preserve

Pickle the bulbs with a basic pickling brine or use in kimchi. You can also dry the whole plant and process it into onion powder. Broth made with wild onion can be frozen.

Future Harvests

Wild onion is not as common as field garlic. Do not overharvest the plant. If you dig up the plant, do it where it is surrounded by other wild onion plants. If you just clip the green tops off, they will regrow, ensuring a long harvest.

Warning

Nothing that smells like onions is poisonous. However, some other members of the lily family are poisonous, and can look like onion plants. The most dangerous look-alike is fly poison (*Amianthium muscaetoxicum*), which has an onionlike bulb that grows into a smooth stem topped with white to green, six-petaled flowers that grow in vertical clusters along the stem. This plant is extremely toxic! Do not even touch it! Other poisonous lilies include death camas (*Zigadenus* species).

wild pear

Pyrus pyraster

EDIBLE fruit

Wild pear is the ancestor of the modern pear. It has small, gritty-textured but delicious fruit.

How to Identify

Wild pear is a tree growing up to 60 feet tall. It has dark, thorny branches. It looks a lot like an apple tree, but is taller and narrower, with finely toothed, elliptical leaves 1½ to 3 inches long. The flowers are cream-white, 1 to 2 inches wide, and produce small, round or pear-shaped fruit.

Where and When to Gather

Wild pear trees grow in open woods, at the edge of forests, and along fencerows. Start checking on the pears in September. They usually do not ripen until early November. The fruit takes a long time to ripen.

The fruit of a wild pear tree is small.

The leaves and flowers of wild pear look just like those of a cultivated pear tree.

How to Gather

Gather the fruit off the ground after a storm has knocked them down.

How to Eat

Wild pears are not very good to eat out of hand. They are extremely gritty. But you can use them to make infused liqueurs and pear brandy.

How to Preserve

Wild pears store just like their domesticated cousins. Keep them in a cool location or even better in a refrigerator for several months to become softer.

Future Harvests

Wild pear is fairly rare. If you come across a tree, you are very lucky. The tree does not depend on its fruit to come back every year, so there is no need to limit your harvest.

wild plum

Prunus americana

EDIBLE fruit

Wild plums are just as delicious as cultivated plums, and can be used in the same way.

How to Identify

Wild plum is a tall shrub or small tree, 6 to 20 feet high, which often forms thickets. Some wild plums have thorns on their twigs. All plums have alternate, 2- to 5-inch-long leaves that are oval to lance-shaped and have serrated margins. The flowers bloom in sparse clusters of two to five, and are ½ to 1 inch across. They have five white or sometimes pink petals. They bloom in very early spring before the leaves appear. Wild plum fruit has a whitish coating called a bloom, just like cultivated plums. The fruit is usually smaller than the cultivated version, and may be yellow, orange, red, or purple-blue. Each fruit contains one large seed.

Where and When to Gather

Wild plums grow in full to partial sun and love abandoned fields and roadsides. They also grow in hollows and open woodlands.

The fruit of this wild plum tree is not ripe yet. The fruit will turn a dark red when ripe.

The pale pink flowers of this wild plum tree are in full bloom.

Collect the ripe fruit from August to October.

How to Gather

When the fruit is ripe, it will come off the tree without any tugging. The best harvest method depends on your end use for the fruit. If you intend to mash the pulp into a purée, lay down a tarp and shake the fruit onto it for a quick harvest of quantity. However, ripe plums will bruise and may split open when they hit the ground. I usually just pick them by hand.

How to Eat

The flavor of wild plums is more tart than the cultivated fruit. Much of the sourness is in the slightly tough skins. If you want just the sweet part of the fruit, first remove the pits, then press the plums through a food mill to remove the skins. The resulting purée can be used to make jam, sauces, and jelly. Personally, I love the sourness of the skins. The plums can be salted and pickled like umeboshi plums in Japan. They can also be used to make plum vinegar.

How to Preserve

Plums can be canned or made into jam, jelly, wine, and vinegar. They can also be salted and pickled.

Future Harvests

You can collect all the fruit you want.

wild rice

Zizania aquatica

EDIBLE seeds

Everyone is familiar with store-bought "wild rice." But did you know that wild rice grows all over the Southeast in shallow freshwater? The flavor of wild rice purchased from a grocery store pales in comparison to wild rice harvested from the wild. The wild flavor is nuttier and deeper.

How to Identify

Wild rice is a tall, erect, annual grass growing up to 10 feet tall in freshwater. The plant grows in clumps of several stout stems, with large, soft, flat leaves growing up to 48 inches long and 2 inches wide. The flowers grow in a cluster (panicle), with a compound branching pattern, from an elongated stalk. The lower branches of the flower cluster bear the drooping male spikelets, while the upper branches bear the female spikelets, which develop into elongated grains.

Another type of edible wild rice, southern wild rice (*Zizaniopsis miliacea*), also grows in the Southeast. It is sometimes called giant cutgrass. The leaves are similar to those of *Zizania aquatica*, but the flower cluster droops and is not separated into male and female flowers. The grains of southern wild rice are much smaller.

Where and When to Gather

Wild rice grows in tidal freshwater and brackish marshes, shallow ponds and lakes, rivers, and nontidal marshes. It is usually found in water 1 to 3 feet deep, but it will grow in water up to 5 feet deep. Clean, clear water with a slow current is important to the growth of wild rice because the grains have very little stored energy compared to tubers or rhizomes of aquatic perennials. A wild rice seedling needs to receive enough sunlight to photosynthesize.

Most people think of harvesting wild rice in the fall. It actually is ready to harvest in late summer. Start looking for patches or fields of it in early August. Look for husks that are full, and grains that are small and green. You also want to be sure that there is a good quantity of rice kernels that can be harvested in a location or you will be wasting your time. Wild rice usually ripens in late August to early September. There are a great many factors affecting when wild rice ripens—the temperature of the water, the current, how short or tall a plant is, and the type of mud all contribute.

Wild rice often grows in a tidal freshwater marsh.

How to Gather

To harvest wild rice, you need several things to get started. You will need a canoe, a paddle or pole, a pair of knocking sticks, a tarp, and some sacks. Any canoe or square-stem skiff will work. I prefer to use a pole rather than a paddle to maneuver through fields of rice. The pole should be lightweight and at least 10 feet long. Cedar is the best wood for poles because of its light weight and durability.

Knocking sticks are one of the most important pieces of equipment for gathering wild rice. When starting out, you can use small branches cut from saplings. If you get more serious about gathering wild rice, I highly recommend making your own sticks from cedar. Knocking sticks are about the size of really long drumsticks or half the length of a pool cue and light-weight but sturdy. A tarp is used to completely cover the bottom of your canoe and some of the sides. The tarp should also be completely free of sand and dirt. The sacks are used to hold the rice you harvest. They should be fairly large and extremely clean. You don't want sand or dirt in your rice.

Ideally, you should have a two-person team for harvesting wild rice. One person uses the pole to keep the canoe moving forward through the rice and the knocker sits in the front, facing backward to "knock" the rice into the canoe. Harvesting wild rice is all about teamwork. When knocking, on your right side, reach out with your stick in your right hand and use it to gently bend the rice stalks toward the canoe. Make sure to connect around the middle of the stalk and not close to the seed head. Then, using the stick in your left hand, gently tap the seed heads. This should happen within moments of touching the stalk with your right stick.

Both sticks should work in unison. Do not worry if you have a hard time at first. You will get the rhythm down in time. Remember, the canoe should be moving while you "knock" the grain into the canoe. The knocking motion should be fast but not violent. If you are breaking stalks while knocking, you are doing it wrong. The wild rice you harvest does not look like the finished product. It is commonly called green rice or the "fuzzy green monster." You should be able to collect at least a bushel in a day.

Wild rice, like other grains, is protected by chaff that must be removed before eating. Processing green rice to get it ready to cook is commonly called "finishing." To "finish" wild rice, it must be dried, parched to make the chaff brittle, rubbed to loosen the chaff from the kernel, and winnowed to remove the chaff (see Winnowing Seeds and Grain, page 18). Finishing wild rice is labor-intensive. For an extremely detailed, step-by-step description of how to finish wild rice, I recommend Samuel Thayer's book *The Forager's Harvest*.

How to Eat

Wild rice cooks in less time than cultivated wild rice. My favorite way to eat wild rice is simply as a side dish seasoned with salt, pepper, and butter. Wild rice can also be used in soups and stews.

How to Preserve

Wild rice will keep as long as it remains dry, but it tastes better if you eat it within a month or two. Always store wild rice in a container that is mouse- and insect-proof.

Future Harvests

Responsible harvesting of wild rice does not affect the life cycle of the plant.

wild strawberry

Fragaria virginiana

`EDIBLE` fruit

The wild strawberries in the Southeast are what you dream of finding when you forage. They are the most intense-tasting strawberries you will ever eat.

How to Identify

Wild strawberry (*Fragaria virginiana*) is a perennial in the rose family. It grows throughout the Southeast and is 2 to 6 inches tall with oval leaves that are coarsely toothed and 1 to 4 inches long. The flowers are white with five petals, each on its own stalk. The plants spread by producing runners. The fruit is much smaller than its cultivated counterparts, usually no bigger than a nickel.

Woodland strawberry (*Fragaria vesca*) is often mistaken for Virginia strawberry in the Southeast, but it has yellow blooms, and seeds stand out from the surface of the fruit. It is edible, but tasteless.

Wild strawberries are starting to bloom in this overgrown field.

Where and When to Gather

Wild strawberries like to grow in open, sunny places. They can be found in fields, at the edges of woods, and along roads. Wild strawberries are around for two weeks and then they are done. When they start to bloom, watch them carefully.

How to Gather

Gather the berries anytime they are ripe. Strawberries do not ripen after you pick them.

How to Eat

Ripe wild strawberries are best used fresh, plain, as is.

How to Preserve

The ripe wild strawberries can be made into jam or infused in alcohol. The unripe strawberries can be pickled or made into a compote.

Future Harvests

There is no need to limit your harvest. You will never be able to pick all of them. Wild strawberries are a hardy perennial and come back year after year.

wineberry

Rubus phoenicolasius

EDIBLE fruit

A friend first told me about these small but delicious red berries, which have a sweet-tart raspberrylike flavor and grow high up in the Appalachian Mountains.

How to Identify

Wineberry produces arching canes as long as 8 feet that can form dense thickets. Instead of the thorns that blackberries and raspberries have, wineberries have hairy bristles that are orange-colored if the plant is growing in full sun but closer to green if growing in part shade. The three-part leaves are toothed; the upper surface is green but the underside is white. The five-petaled flowers are white, less than 1 inch across, and grow in loose clusters. Wineberries are compound fruits like raspberries, but orange-red in color.

The wineberry bush bears small fruit that is red when ripe.

Where and When to Gather

Wineberries grow in full to part sun or occasionally even in part shade. Look for wineberry along roadsides, in parks, and at the edge of fields and clearings. Wineberries are in season in June and July.

How to Gather

When picking wineberries, put them in a container rather than a bag so that the soft berries don't get smashed in transport.

How to Eat

Wineberries are best eaten fresh. Use them on desserts and in fruit salads. They can also be made into sauces.

How to Preserve

Make jam, jelly, vinegar, and wine from wineberries.

Future Harvests

There is no need to limit your harvest.

wintergreen

Gaultheria procumbens

EDIBLE leaves, berries

Wintergreen tastes and smells like wintergreen chewing gum but with a much cleaner flavor.

How to Identify

Wintergreen is a low-growing evergreen with leathery, oval, mildly toothed leaves, 1 to 2 inches long. In the colder months, the leaves may turn partially or completely red. The flowers are white and bell-shaped, and dangle from the upper leaf axils in midsummer. The tips of the bells have five small lobes. The berries are red, less than ½ inch wide, and can persist on the plants from when they first ripen in fall to the following spring. The whole plant has a minty aroma when crushed.

Where and When to Gather

Wintergreen is a woodland plant that grows in full to partial shade in moist, acidic soils.

Crush the leaves with your hand to release the wintergreen fragrance of the leaves.

The leaves can be gathered year-round. Gather the ripe berries from fall to winter.

How to Gather
Snap off the top few inches of the stalks, leaves and berries attached. You can use scissors or shears. Do not take everything from a patch of wintergreen, just a little bit here, a little bit there.

How to Eat
Infuse the leaves by pouring hot water over them and steep at room temperature for three to five days. You can make a simple syrup with the infused water. Leaf-infused wintergreen hard alcohol beverages are excellent. The berries are good raw in small amounts with yogurt, in ice cream or sorbet, and in smoothies.

How to Preserve
Wintergreen syrup or infused alcoholic drinks are the best way to preserve this plant.

Future Harvests
Never pull up the whole plant. By sustainably harvesting the plant, you will let it regrow and persist.

wisteria

Wisteria frutescens
American wisteria

EDIBLE flowers

Many people think of wisteria as just a lovely, fragrant flower of spring. It is, but the flowers are edible.

How to Identify

Wisteria is a climbing, woody vine with smooth bark that grows 6 to 30 feet long. The alternate, oval leaves grow 2 inches long. The flowers form drooping clusters with petals that are purple to lilac.

Where and When to gather

Wisteria grows at the edge of woods, along streams, and in thickets. It blooms in early spring, April to May, and lasts for a few weeks.

The showy blooms of wisteria are uniquely fragrant.

How to Gather

Gather wisteria flowers anytime the plant is blooming. Rain will wash the flavor out. Only gather the flowers.

How to Eat

The flowers can be eaten raw or cooked. They have a sweet, floral fragrance. Use them in salads or infuse them into liquids.

How to Preserve

Infuse the flowers into liquids. The sweet, floral fragrance works well infused into syrups.

Future Harvests

There is no need to limit your harvest. Wisteria is an invasive vine that lives for a very long time.

Warning

The flowers are the only edible part of the plant. Everything else is extremely poisonous.

wood nettle

Laportea canadensis

EDIBLE leaves, stem

Wood nettles sting just like stinging nettle. They can also be eaten in the same manner. The leaves and stems can be eaten like any fresh green. The taste is a deep, herbal flavor.

How to Identify

Wood nettle is a perennial growing 2 to 4 feet tall. The green, serrated, ovate leaves grow 2½ to 8 inches long on leafstalks. Tiny, greenish flowers grow in long dangly threads from leaf axils. Wood nettle has stinging hairs on the stem and leaves. The two main differences between wood nettle and stinging nettle are that the leaves of wood nettle are larger and the plants are shorter.

Where and When to Gather

Wood nettle grows in damp, rich woods by streams. Gather the leaves of wood nettle in the spring before the plant starts to flower.

Wood nettle grows by streams in open woods.

How to Gather

Wood nettle will sting you if you touch it with bare hands. Always wear gloves when harvesting and use scissors to cut the leaf-stalks with leaves attached.

How to Eat

Wood nettle is excellent in soups, sauces, pestos, quiches, teas, and as a side dish. The stinging magically disappears when the leaves and stems are cooked or dried.

How to Preserve

Dry the leaves and stems by wrapping a rubber band around a bunch of wood nettle and hanging the bundle upside down in a dry, airy place until completely dry. Crumble and store in an airtight container. Dried wood nettle makes an excellent tea. You can also make pesto with the leaves and freeze it.

Future Harvests

Only harvest from well-established patches, and cut the stalks so the plant regrows.

wood sorrel

Oxalis stricta

EDIBLE leaves, stems, flowers, seedpods

I see wood sorrel growing in the city and out in the country. It comes up in garden beds, sidewalks, and any place where there is bare soil. I love it for its lemony, sour flavor, which should have a place in every summertime salad.

How to Identify

Wood sorrel is a perennial in the genus *Oxalis*. It has small, three-part, heart-shaped leaves that look like clover but different. The leaves grow on slender stems to 8 inches tall, and the plant has yellow flowers.

There are no poisonous look-alikes. Often times, clover or common phlox is mistaken for wood sorrel. Common phlox has pinkish purple flowers and grows into a dome shape. Clover has pom-pom–shaped or elongated pom-pom flowers.

Wood sorrel grows all summer long.

Where and When to Gather

Wood sorrel grows anywhere there is disturbed soil. It starts appearing in late spring as sheep sorrel is on the decline, and grows until late summer.

How to Gather

Gather wood sorrel until it starts to get tough in late summer. The stems, leaves, flowers, and seedpods are edible.

How to Eat

Wood sorrel is best eaten raw. It is tasty in salads and as a garnish. You can also infuse it into liquids.

How to Preserve

Wood sorrel can be infused into a liquid or juice and frozen.

Future Harvests

Even though wood sorrel is plentiful, never take everything. Always cut just some with scissors to ensure it grows back.

yarrow

Achillea millefolium

EDIBLE leaves, flowers

Yarrow is a powerful medicinal herb that can help heal cuts quickly. It is also an edible with a sweet and pungent flavor.

How to Identify

Yarrow's leaves are so finely divided that they are featherlike. The basal leaves have leafstalks and can grow up to 6 inches long and 1 inch wide, with alternate upper leaves that are stalkless but still divided and feathery and as small as 1 inch long. People frequently confuse yarrow's flat, white flower clusters with wild carrot flowers. But if you look at yarrow's small individual flowers rather than the whole lacy group of them, you'll see that each has a distinct round center area made up of numerous disk flowers. And yarrow is not as tall; it grows up to 2 feet tall, while wild carrot grows 4 to 5 feet tall.

Where and When to Gather

Yarrow grows in full sun to partial shade, but you'll find that it has a stronger flavor growing in full sun as opposed to woodland settings. The roadside plants are usually

Yarrow often grows by the roadside.

much smaller, sometimes only a few inches tall, whereas in moist meadows, yarrow can grow up to 3 feet high. The best time to collect yarrow is in the summer.

How to Gather

Snap by hand or use scissors to cut off the upper few inches of stem with leaves and flowers attached.

How to Eat

The flavor of yarrow is complex—sweet and pungent. To brew yarrow tea, pour boiling hot water over the fresh or dried flowers and leaves, cover, and let steep for ten minutes before straining. Sweeten with honey, if you like. Use the fresh or dried leaves as a seasoning for savory dishes. Chefs also sometimes use the leaves as a garnish or in salads.

How to Preserve

Dry yarrow leaves and flowers by bundling eight to ten stalks together and hanging them upside down away from direct light or heat. In about a week, the stalks should be dry enough so that you can easily crumble the leaves and flowers off the stems. Store in an airtight jar.

Future Harvests

There is no need to limit your harvest. Always make sure to cut the leaves so that the plant can regrow.

yellow trout lily

Erythronium americanum

trout lily, yellow dogtooth violet, fawn lily, adder's tongue

EDIBLE flowers, corms

The speckled leaves of yellow trout lily will catch your attention with their unique appearance when you are walking in the woods. The corms are crisp, chewy, and taste like sweet corn or snow peas.

How to Identify

Yellow trout lily is a perennial plant that grows up to 9 inches tall. It has two green elliptical leaves that grow 4 to 6 inches long. The leaves are mottled purple-brown, reminiscent of the markings of brown or brook trout. The nodding flowers are yellow with red spots inside. The lily comes up in fertile woods from an underground bulb, or corm. Sometimes you will find them blooming in colonies, which is a breathtaking sight.

There are several different trout lilies. Yellow trout lily is the most common

Yellow trout lily has mottled leaves and a yellow flower.

species in the Southeast. Trout lily roots retrieve phosphorus from the soil and transfer it to their leaves, and so deer love to eat the leaves.

Where and When to Gather
Yellow trout lily grows in fertile, moist woods. The leaves start appearing in early to mid-spring and grow until summer.

How to Gather
Gather yellow trout lily corms by digging them up in the spring. Harvest the leaves by cutting.

How to Eat
The corms are the best part of the plant. They can be eaten raw or cooked. My favorite use of the corms is to add them at the end of a stir-fry so they retain their texture and don't get overcooked.

How to Preserve
After harvesting, keep the plant parts with a damp paper towel in an airtight container in the refrigerator. The corms can be pickled to extend the harvest.

Future Harvests
There are only two leaves per plant, so harvest sparingly. Take plants only from where there are several more. Yellow trout lily takes a long time to grow.

Further reading

Brill, "Wildman" Steve, and Evelyn Dean. *Identifying and Harvesting Edible and Medicinal Plants in Wild (and Not So Wild) Places*. New York: William Morrow, 1994. Also see his website, wildmansteve-brill.com.

Horn, Dennis, and Tavia Cathcart. *Wildflowers of Tennessee, the Ohio Valley, and the Southern Appalachians*. Auburn, WA: Lone Pine Publishing, 2013.

Kallas, Dr. John. *Edible Wild Plants: Wild Foods from Dirt to Plate*. Layton, UT: Gibbs Smith, 2010. Also see his website, wildfoodadventures.com.

Kirkman, Katherine L., Claud L. Brown, and Donald J. Leopold. *Native Trees of the Southeast: An Identification Guide*. Portland, OR: Timber Press, 2007.

Thayer, Sam. *The Forager's Harvest: A Guide to Identifying, Harvesting, and Preparing Edible Wild Plants*. New York: HarperCollins, 2006. Also see his website, foragersharvest.com.

Thayer, Sam. *Nature's Garden: A Guide to Identifying, Harvesting, and Preparing Edible Wild Plants*. Birchwood, WI: Forager's Harvest Press, 2010. Also see his website, foragersharvest.com.

Tiner, Ralph W. *Field Guide to Coastal Wetland Plants of the Southeastern United States*. Amherst: University of Massachusetts Press, 1993.

Acknowledgments

I would like to thank Leda Meredith for helping me out in so many ways before, during, and after writing this book. She was invaluable! I also would like to thank my family and Kathryn Abrams for their support. The following people also helped make this book happen: Chris Hastings, Jeremiah Langhorne, Daniel Heinze, Edwin Bloodworth, Jason Horn, Melina Hammer, Michelle Reynolds, Megan Gremelspacher, Katie Davis, Grant Brigham, and Cecile Brigham.

Much appreciation to all who contributed photos, and especially Bob Farley, Leda Meredith, Lisa M. Rose, and Hank Shaw.

A huge thank-you to all the staff at Timber Press and to my copyeditor, Ellen Wheat.

Photography Credits

Donald Cameron, page 50

Glen Mittelhauser, pages 221, 222

Hank Shaw, pages 33, 35

Karie Reinertson, page 269

Leda Meredith, pages 34, 48, 59 right, 64, 81, 89, 91, 99, 101, 102, 104, 105, 106, 108, 114, 116, 126, 130, 141, 142, 146, 154, 162, 171, 176, 184, 186, 189, 200, 205, 209, 213, 229, 238, 243, 247, 251

Lisa M. Rose, pages 2, 17, 21, 28, 39, 52 left, 60, 124, 144, 148, 207, 281

Mark A. Garland @ USDA-NRCS PLANTS Database, page 164

Robert Farley, pages 129, 193, 194, 203, 225, 232, 245

Bugwood.org

Chris Evans, Illinois Wildlife Action Plan, page 134 right

David Stephens, page 263

Graves Lovell, Alabama Department of Conservation and Natural Resources, page 265

Howard F. Schwartz, Colorado State University, page 262

Montana Statewide Noxious Weed Awareness and Education Program Archive, Montana State University, page 179

Rebekah D. Wallace, University of Georgia, page 211

Rob Routledge, Sault College, pages 69, 95, 181 top

Troy Evans, Great Smoky Mountains National Park, page 181 bottom

Wendy VanDyk Evans, page 53

Flickr

bobistraveling, page 240

Dendroica cerulea, page 136

IndiePhoto, page 135

Mr. Tonreg, page 249

Nicholas A. Tonelli, page 57

Superior National Forest, page 31

iStockphoto

Joe Potato, page 152

zig4photo, page 44

Wikimedia

A Engelhardt, page 151

Beentree, 160

Circeus, 168

Dcrjsr, 204

H. Zell, pages 74, 173

Leitpeter (Peter Leitheiser), page 241

Marco Vinicio Olla, page 120

Matt Lavin, page 112

MONGO, page 67 top

Nova, page 83

PhytoplanktonSandwich, page 191

Velella, page 150

All other photos are by the author.

Index

About the Author

CARY NORTON

Chris Bennett is a forager, writer, teacher, cheesemonger, and trained chef. He is the cheesemonger for Whole Foods in Birmingham, Alabama, and enjoys working with top chefs in the area to provide wild edibles for their restaurants. He has been featured in *Birmingham* magazine, *Cooking Light*, and *The Hot and Hot Fish Club Cookbook*. He is a frequent speaker at various venues, having presented sessions at the Atlanta and Charleston Food and Wine Festivals. He has also blogged for *Garden and Gun* magazine (gardenandgun.com). Chris offers workshops on seasonal wild edibles at Hollow Spring Farm, his family's farm in Pell City, Alabama, leading eager participants with adventurous palates to graze on wild riches.